"The Conservative Holiness Movement owes a debt of gratitude to the faculty of God's Bible School and College for focusing attention on the crucial issues we face through *The Call to the Conservative Holiness Movement.* The subsequent essays of Michael Avery and Larry Smith carefully delineate the problem areas that confront us but also carefully lead us to suggested remedies that provide a window of opportunity for the renewing of our conservative churches and organizations. You probably won't agree with everything the authors have written, but you can't help but be challenged by *The Call.*"

—**Leonard Sankey**, General Secretary, Interchurch Holiness Convention

"Revival and renewal almost always begin with self-examination and confession, and *The Call* is so serious, insightful (and even painful) that it just might be God's way of starting a fresh holiness movement for the future. I pray so."

—**Keith Drury**, church leader, author, Associate Professor, Indiana Wesleyan University

"There are many 'calls' clamoring for our attention. *The Call to the Conservative Holiness Movement* is one that must have it!"

—**Rodney Loper**, Senior Pastor, Hobe Sound Bible Church

"You will argue with the writers of *The Call* that these pages are not a portrait of you, your church, or our movement. But after a while, I trust we will be led to pray with Isaiah, 'We have failed … change us … send us again.'"

—**David Eslinger**, Tulsa, Oklahoma, development engineer

"*The Call* is a powerful, articulate, and courageously written body of material. If we will honestly use this information as a tool of the Spirit, it will enable us to live, walk, and minister with greater clarity and effectiveness."

—**G. Clair Sams**, President, Heartland Conference, Bible Methodist Connection

"I heartily recommend *The Call*. It is a call to unity, not uniformity; to the 'principle within'; to the fervent evangelizing of the lost; and to discipling one another. May *The Call* become a magnetic center to unite and mobilize us!"

—**Timothy L. Cooley, Sr.**, Academic Dean, Penn View Bible Institute

THE CALL

Essays to the Conservative Holiness Movement

THE CALL

Essays to the Conservative Holiness Movement

Revivalist Press
Cincinnati, Ohio

THE CALL

Essays to the Conservative Holiness Movement

ISBN: 978-0-9749186-9-3

publishing ministry of

God's Bible School & College
1810 Young Street
Cincinnati, OH 45202
Revivalist@gbs.edu

Library of Congress Control Number: 2013906134

Printed by Country Pines, Shoals, Indiana
United States of America

Dedication

In honor of those who birthed this Movement and in support of those who will forge its future.

Contents

PREFACE

It was in 2007 that a group of faculty at God's Bible School and College issued a thoughtful document entitled, "A Call to the Conservative Holiness Movement." Its purpose was to encourage renewed commitment to the essentials of scriptural Christianity as the Conservative Holiness Movement (CHM) has received them, as well as to reclaim its heritage as Christians of Wesleyan conviction. This document was printed in its entirety in the October 2011 issue of *God's Revivalist.* In subsequent issues, essays were written to provide both commentary and explanation for each of the ten original articles of the "Call."

These essays, now republished in this book, flow from the belief that we are best serving the movement which we love by raising issues tied directly to our prosperity and perhaps even to our survival? For who can doubt that we are facing an identity crisis that not only questions the validity of our past but also threatens the promise of our future? Doubtless we are witnessing the usual pattern of "historical drift" fueled by increasing affluence and the desire for social respectability that seems to impact most religious structures. Compounding this problem is a narrowness in understanding and a lopsidedness in development that have moved us away from the careful and dynamic balance that is so essential to our legacy as Wesleyans. All this has distorted our witness, leaving us too often without clear understanding or compelling vision for the mission to which Jesus calls us in fruitful ministry to this shattered world.

In these essays we make no claim either to spiritual superiority or to infallible perception. But every word that we have written is offered humbly and prayerfully in earnest hope that our efforts will encourage serious dialogue, as well as renewed commitment to the great foundational principles of our origin.

Michael Avery and Larry Smith
January 18, 2013

A Call To The Conservative Holiness Movement

Published 2007

PROLOGUE

Deeply concerned for the future of the Holiness Movement, and especially of the Conservative Holiness Movement of which we are a part, we issue this call for the full and vigorous recovery of our heritage as Christians of Wesleyan conviction. We share the distress of those who warn of "historical drift," spiritual apathy, and surrender to the depraved secular culture that surrounds us. We submit that a renewed commitment to the essential principles of scriptural Christianity which we have received in classical Methodist belief, piety and mission will prepare and strengthen us for the challenges that confront us. We appeal, therefore, to our entire movement to unite with us joyfully in this commitment, pledging uncompromising faithfulness to God's Word and to creative relevance in our ministry. Upon the original foundations of our movement, therefore, we must build

DETERMINED, EFFECTIVE AND CONTEMPORARY WITNESS TO GOD'S UNCHANGING SUMMONS TO HOLY HEARTS AND HOLY LIVES. WITHOUT PRESUMING TO ADDRESS ALL OUR NEEDS, WE HAVE IDENTIFIED TEN OF THE THEMES TO WHICH WE AS CONSERVATIVE HOLINESS CHRISTIANS MUST GIVE CAREFUL CONSIDERATION.

A CALL TO BIBLICAL FIDELITY

AS WESLEYANS WE AFFIRM THAT THE HOLY SCRIPTURES, AS THE INSPIRED AND INERRANT WORD OF GOD, ARE THE BASIS OF AUTHORITY IN THE CHURCH, NORMATIVE FOR ALL OUR FAITH AND PRACTICE. WE DECLARE WITH THE ENGLISH REFORMERS, "HOLY SCRIPTURE CONTAINS EVERYTHING THAT IS NECESSARY FOR SALVATION, SO THAT WHATEVER IS NOT STATED IN IT, OR CANNOT BE PROVED BY IT, MUST NOT BE REQUIRED OF ANY MAN AS AN ARTICLE OF BELIEF OR BE THOUGHT REQUISITE OR NECESSARY TO SALVATION." YET WE HAVE OFTEN FOCUSED ON ISSUES AND MADE DEMANDS WHICH WE CANNOT LEGITIMATELY ESTABLISH FROM THE SCRIPTURES. AS A RESULT, TRIVIAL NOTIONS AND SPECULATIONS AT TIMES HAVE MARRED OUR WITNESS. WE CALL, THEREFORE, FOR RENEWED SUBMISSION TO THE ABSOLUTE AUTHORITY OF THE BIBLE, NOT AS A REVERED ICON, BUT AS THE TOUCHSTONE FOR BOTH OUR PERSONAL LIVES AND OUR PUBLIC PROCLAMATION. FOR IN EVERY AGE, THE CHURCH MUST SUBMIT ITSELF UNCONDITIONALLY TO THE WORD OF GOD, INTERPRETING IT IN HARMONY WITH ITSELF, IN KEEPING WITH THE BEST INSIGHTS OF HISTORICAL AND LITERARY STUDY, UNDER

THE GUIDANCE OF THE HOLY SPIRIT, AND WITH RESPECT FOR THE HISTORIC UNDERSTANDING OF DEVOUT CHRISTIAN SCHOLARSHIP.

A CALL TO HISTORIC ROOTS AND CONTINUITY

WE GLADLY AFFIRM OUR ALLEGIANCE TO THE CLASSICAL CHRISTIANITY OF THE CENTURIES, CONFESSING ITS FAITH, SHARING ITS HISTORIC WITNESS, LIVING OUT ITS GODLY DISCIPLINE, AND CLAIMING ALL OF ITS TREASURES AS OUR OWN. WE GIVE GOD PRAISE FOR OUR LEGACY OF EVANGELICAL CHRISTIANITY MAGNIFICENTLY SET FORTH IN THE HEROIC LIVES OF ANCIENT CHRISTIANS, THE FAITHFUL WITNESSES OF THE MIDDLE AGES, THE STALWART TESTIMONY OF THE REFORMERS, THE BIBLICAL PROCLAMATION OF THE WESLEYS, AND THE EARNEST PIETY OF THE EARLY HOLINESS MOVEMENT. WE REJOICE IN THE LIVES AND MINISTRY OF EARNEST FOLLOWERS OF OUR LORD FROM EVERY BRANCH OF ORTHODOX CHRISTIANITY. BUT TOO OFTEN WE HAVE SMUGLY DISCONNECTED OURSELVES FROM OUR CHRISTIAN PAST; AND IN SO DOING WE HAVE BECOME THEOLOGICALLY SHALLOW, SPIRITUALLY WEAK AND BLIND TO THE WORK OF GOD IN THE LIVES OF OTHERS. WE HAVE WITHDRAWN OURSELVES INTO PROTECTED ENCLAVES, CONGRATULATING OURSELVES ON OUR SUPERIORITY OVER OTHER CHRISTIANS, SOMETIMES REFUSING FELLOWSHIP WITH THEM BECAUSE OF OUR DISAGREEMENT IN DOCTRINE OR IN PRACTICE, AND IGNORING THE CONTINUING WORK OF THE HOLY SPIRIT THROUGHOUT ALL THE UNIVERSAL CHURCH. AT BEST, THIS IS LAMENTABLE IGNORANCE, AND AT WORST, SEC-

TARIAN BIGOTRY. WE CALL THEREFORE, WITH JOHN WESLEY, FOR A "LEAGUE OFFENSIVE AND DEFENSIVE WITH EVERY SOLDIER OF CHRIST," RECLAIMING THE RICHNESS OF OUR CHRISTIAN HERITAGE AND OUR ESSENTIAL UNITY WITH ALL WHO TRULY CONFESS HIM AS LORD.

A CALL TO CHRISTIAN COMMUNITY

UNION WITH CHRIST ESTABLISHES MEMBERSHIP IN HIS CHURCH, THE COMMUNITY OF THE FAITHFUL, IN ALL TIMES AND PLACES. IT IS FOUNDED BY OUR LORD AND ESTABLISHED UPON HIMSELF, AND WE CLAIM HIS INFALLIBLE PROMISE THAT THE GATES OF HELL SHALL NEVER WITHSTAND IT. AS WE LIVE OUT OUR FAITHFULNESS TO HIM, WE MUST ALSO LIVE IN FAITHFULNESS TO THE CHURCH, WHICH IS HIS BODY AND BRIDE, LIVING AND DYING IN ITS COMMUNION. WE AFFIRM THE TRADITIONAL PROTESTANT INSISTENCE THAT THE VISIBLE CHURCH IS THE CONGREGATION OF THE FAITHFUL IN WHICH THE "PURE WORD OF GOD IS PREACHED AND THE SACRAMENTS DULY ADMINISTERED ACCORDING TO CHRIST'S ORDINANCE." TOO OFTEN, HOWEVER, WE HAVE ADOPTED A NARROW AND INDIVIDUALISTIC APPROACH TO OUR CHRISTIAN FAITH. SOMETIMES WE HAVE SO EMPHASIZED PERSONAL SPIRITUAL RELATIONSHIP THAT WE HAVE FORGOTTEN THAT RELATIONSHIP MUST BE REALIZED, STRENGTHENED AND ADVANCED WITHIN THE COMPANY OF GOD'S PEOPLE. AT OTHER TIMES, WE HAVE IMAGINED THAT WE WERE THE CHURCH, OR AT LEAST THAT THE HOLINESS MOVEMENT WAS ITS MOST SIGNIFICANT COMPONENT RATHER THAN ONLY A TINY SEGMENT OF ITS FELLOWSHIP. WE CALL, THEREFORE, FOR

RENEWED UNDERSTANDING OF THE BIBLICAL DOCTRINE OF THE CHURCH AS "THE PILLAR AND GROUND OF THE TRUTH," REVERENCE FOR ITS ORTHODOX CONFESSIONS, SUBMISSION TO ITS HOLY DISCIPLINE, AND FAITHFULNESS TO ITS COMMON LIFE. AS A COALITION OF HOLINESS BELIEVERS WITHIN ITS COMMUNION, WE GLADLY BUT HUMBLY OFFER OUR GIFTS TO THE UNIVERSAL CHURCH–GIFTS WHICH CENTER IN OUR HISTORIC FOCUS ON HOLINESS OF HEART AND LIFE.

A CALL TO CHRISTIAN HOLINESS

HOLINESS OF HEART AND LIFE FLOWING OUT OF LOVE FOR GOD, AS WE BELIEVE, IS THE "CENTRAL IDEA OF CHRISTIANITY," FOR THIS IS GOD'S REDEMPTIVE PURPOSE FOR OUR FALLEN HUMANITY. HOLINESS IS BOTH HIS GIFT AND OUR PURSUIT, AND AS THE WRITER TO HEBREWS REMINDS US, WITHOUT IT NONE OF US SHALL EVER SEE THE LORD. NEGATIVELY, HOLINESS IS SEPARATION FROM ALL THAT IS SINFUL AND UNLIKE CHRIST; AND POSITIVELY, SEPARATION UNTO GODLINESS, RIGHTEOUSNESS AND FULL CHRISTLIKENESS. IT BEGINS IN REGENERATION BY THE SPIRIT, FLOURISHES IN THE WORK OF ENTIRE SANCTIFICATION, AND ADVANCES THROUGHOUT OUR LIVES. AS WESLEYANS, WE REASSERT THE BIBLICAL PASSION OF OUR FOREBEARS "TO REFORM THE CONTINENT AND SPREAD SCRIPTURAL HOLINESS OVER THESE LANDS."

WE CONFESS, HOWEVER, THAT OUR PASSION FOR HOLINESS OF HEART AND LIFE HAS SOMETIMES BEEN REDUCED MERELY TO EXTERNAL CODES AND PROHIBITIONS, AND "HOLIER-THAN-THOU" ATTITUDES TOWARD THOSE WHO DIFFER FROM US. AS SUCH WE HAVE become shell without substance, and betrayed the Scriptural mandate to be holy, because the Lord our God is holy. We therefore call our Movement to a renewed love for God from which will blossom consistent and winsome lives of holiness–first, in motivating purpose; and second, in outward conduct. This means that we must continue to accentuate both of the definitive moments we identify as works of divine grace, conversion and entire sanctification, all the while giving proper attention to the progressive growth in grace by the Spirit and the increasing separation from the world which our Methodist forebears so firmly stressed.

A CALL TO METHODIST PIETY

Our Methodist heritage has underscored the necessity of devout personal piety grounded in sincere love and profound reverence for God. This implies binding and lifelong covenant with Him, living faith in Christ our great sin bearer, allegiance to the inner principle of "jealous godly fear," commitment to disciplined discipleship, faithful obedience to His holy Law, dynamic growth in grace, and faithful use of the means of grace. All holiness of heart and life must be grounded in sober and steadfast love for God.

Sometimes, however, our emphasis on external regulation and dutiful performance has ignored the principles of authentic piety. Our appeals to holy conduct, which are both legitimate and necessary, have often been based more in the impulse to preserve the taboos of our religious subculture than in allegiance to the Word of God and its demands. The heart of all Christian obligation is loving God with all our heart, soul and mind; and then "to fear Him and keep His commandments." Not only are we called to do what is right but also to love what is right, for this reason abstaining from all that He condemns and embracing all that He enjoins. We will never stop the "historical drift" among us merely by enforcing traditional legislation but by vigorous and renewed insistence upon authentic relationship with God and passionate pursuit of Him. Gladly we reaffirm our traditional emphasis upon simplicity, modesty, stewardship, separation from the world and conscientious lifestyle, but all this must be within this warm and gracious context of loving what God loves and hating what God hates.

As Methodists, therefore, we call our Movement to return to our originating commitment to principled covenant with God. Which, according to the General Rules of 1743, demanded these commitments: (1) the renunciation of all known sin, (2) the embracing of all positive virtue, and (3) the faithful practice of the means of grace, especially "the instituted means of grace," defined as the Word, prayer, fasting, Christian fellowship and the Lord's Supper. This demands disciplined life within the community of the Church; a renewing of our historic pattern of spiritual formation through small accountability groups, such as the class meeting; and faithful submission to healthy and holy discipline, while at the same time we are altogether dependent upon the gracious work of the Spirit who changes us "from glory to glory" into the likeness of Our Lord.

A CALL TO AUTHORITY IN THE CHURCH

Christ Our Lord has delegated the powers of government to duly appointed officers in the Church, and we are mandated to obey them faithfully. All Christians are to be in practical submission to one another and to these designated officials in the Church. The edifying and equipping of God's people and the administration of church discipline are committed especially to faithful pastors who are called not as "lords over God's heritage," but as examples and as shepherds of His flock.

We therefore deplore the spirit of autonomy and even anarchy which so often has marked our Movement. Too often in our congregations and denominational life we have exhibited rebellion against the authority structures which God Himself has established, boasting our independence of them, and refusing to submit to their godly discipline. This has been evidenced by continuing divisions among us, often over matters unconnected with allegiance to Scriptural truth. As the heirs of classical Christianity, we have not so learned Christ. "Obey them that have the rule over you, and submit yourselves: for they watch for your souls as they that must give account, that they may do it with joy, and not with grief: for that is unprofitable to you" (Heb. 13:17).

We call therefore for renewed exposition of the Scriptural qualifications for leadership within the Church, corporate exhortation to beware the deceitfulness of sin, and Biblical obedience and submission to those whom God has made under shepherds over us. God grants no Christian autonomy from mutual submission and accountability within the Body of Christ. We must therefore repent of our oft refusals to exercise the Scriptural means of restorative discipline within the Church and commit ourselves to loving one another even as our Father loves us in chastening and scourging every son whom He receives.

A CALL TO CORPORATE WORSHIP

Corporate worship is the exalted glory and central pulse of every Christian congregation. At its core, worship is the adoration of God: Holy, Blessed, and Undivided Trinity; and by apostolic mandate, it is to be conducted with decency and order. In the public worship of the Church, as the old Methodist communion service reminds us, we join "angels and archangels and all the company of heaven [to] laud and magnify" the Lord of hosts, joining in their eternal hymn, "Holy, Holy, Holy, Lord God of hosts, Heaven and earth are full of Thy glory."

As Wesleyans we have a twofold heritage in Christian worship. On the one hand is the warmth and earnestness of fervent and joyful devotion. On the other is the sober restraint of form, dignity and tradition. Both are essential. Too often, however, we have emphasized the first and neglected the second. We need not neglect the subjective emphasis so characteristic of our services, but we must ground our sacrifices of praise and thanksgiving in the great objective acts and truths of God Himself.

We call therefore for the renewal of our corporate worship, based in the mandates of Scripture and in the tradition of evangelical orthodoxy, centered in the faithful ministry of Word and Sacrament. Our preaching must be based in conscientious interpretation and earnest proclamation of the Holy Scriptures; and our administration of the sacred ordinances of baptism and the Lord's Supper must be meaningful and faithful. We lament our neglect of baptism and the Lord's Table, for this is to slight the Savior who so kindly has established them to fortify our faith, calm our fears and nourish us with grace.

A CALL TO CONSISTENT DISCIPLESHIP

Christ commissioned His followers to make disciples through Trinitarian baptism and instruction in all His commands. The early church responded to Our Lord's call to aggressive evangelism by taking the gospel to every corner of their world. Yet they realized that the central thrust of the Great Commission was dis-

CIPLESHIP ACCOMPLISHED THROUGH BAPTISM AND TEACHING, SO THEY LARGELY INVESTED THEIR TIME AND ENERGY IN SYSTEMATICALLY TEACHING NEW CONVERTS THE WHOLE COUNSEL OF GOD AND EQUIPPING THEM FOR MINISTRY. THIS SAME EMPHASIS ELEVATED WESLEYAN METHODISM TO TOWERING STATURE IN THE KINGDOM OF GOD, WHILE WITHOUT IT WHITEFIELDIAN METHODISM PROVED "A ROPE OF SAND." WE CONFESS THAT, DESPITE OUR HERITAGE, EVANGELISM HAS LANGUISHED AMONG US. WE HAVE LARGELY ABANDONED OUR METHODIST SYSTEM OF SPIRITUAL FORMATION AND FORGOTTEN HOW TO FULFILL OUR LORD'S COMMAND TO MAKE DISCIPLES. WE HAVE SOUGHT REVIVAL WITHOUT PREPARING TO PRESERVE ITS FRUITS. WE HAVE EMPHASIZED SPECTACULAR CONVERSIONS AND NEGLECTED THE BIBLICAL NECESSITY OF DISCIPLINED GROWTH IN FAITH, VIRTUE, KNOWLEDGE, SELF-CONTROL, PERSEVERANCE, GODLINESS, BROTHERLY KINDNESS AND LOVE. WE FURTHER ACKNOWLEDGE THAT WHERE EVANGELISM IS TAKING PLACE AMONG US, A SYSTEMATIC PLAN FOR INCORPORATING NEW CONVERTS INTO THE VISIBLE BODY OF CHRIST THROUGH BAPTISM AND INSTRUCTION IS LARGELY NONEXISTENT.

WE CALL, THEREFORE, NOT MERELY FOR A REAFFIRMATION OF THE IMPORTANCE OF EVANGELISM AND DISCIPLESHIP, BUT FOR A COMMITMENT TO EQUIP OUR LAITY FOR THE WORK OF THE MINISTRY, FOR THE ESTABLISHMENT OF SOLIDLY WESLEYAN CURRICULA FOR SYSTEMATIC DISCIPLESHIP, AND FOR THE IMPLEMENTATION OF THESE TRAINING METHODS IN ALL OUR CHURCHES. THIS WILL NECESSITATE A CONCERTED EFFORT ON THE PART OF OUR LEADERS TO RECLAIM THE SKILLS OF DISCIPLESHIP, REINSTITUTE REGULAR SYSTEMS OF ACCOUNTability and affirmation, and to resume obedience to Scripture's mandate to teach faithful men who shall be able to teach others also. We shall begin again to bear much fruit when our disciples themselves become disciple makers.

A Call to Christian Social Witness

Our Lord's call to take up the cross and follow Him is a call to Christian social witness, for everywhere the Master went He ministered to both the spiritual and physical needs of people. We have been created in Christ Jesus for good works (Eph. 2:10). Indeed, saving faith works through love (Gal. 5:6)–first in meeting the needs of fellow believers, and second in doing good to all men. Love for Our Lord and passion for holiness should impel us to minister compassionately to the sick, the suffering and the forsaken, and to resist courageously societal structures that oppose divine purpose and degrade human dignity. "Whenever the Christian lives an authentic life, the world around is permeated with God's presence...," as Dr. Leon Hynson has written. "[He] raises the quality of life, makes social justice, equity and integrity work. The pure in heart not only 'see' God, but become the letters through which society sees Him."

Unfortunately, we have sometimes withdrawn from that society into the cloistered walls of a narrow and narcissistic piety. But this was not the pattern of our spiritual fore-

BEARS WHO RAISED CHRISTIAN CONSCIOUSNESS IN ALL THE FORUMS OF PUBLIC LIFE AND WHO FILLED THEIR LAND WITH WORKS OF GRACE AND MERCY. THEIR STATED MISSION, "TO REFORM THE CONTINENT AND SPREAD SCRIPTURAL HOLINESS OVER THESE LANDS" ASSERTED GOD'S SANCTIFYING PURPOSE TO TRANSFORM LIVES AND IN CONSEQUENCE TO TRANSFORM CULTURE.

WE CALL THEREFORE FOR RENEWED COMMITMENT TO CHRISTIAN SOCIAL WITNESS. THIS MEANS THAT WE WILL LOVINGLY AND FORCEFULLY PROCLAIM CHRIST'S POWER TO LIBERATE FROM SIN, BOTH PUBLIC AND PRIVATE, ASSERTING THE CLAIMS OF HIS KINGDOM AGAINST ALL THAT MILITATES AGAINST IT. THIS COMMITMENT WILL ALSO LEAD US TO MINISTER COMPASSIONATELY IN HIS NAME TO THE IMPRISONED, THE NEEDY AND THE OPPRESSED.

A CALL TO RESURGENT HOPE

ALL CHRISTIAN LIFE IS CENTERED IN THE RESPLENDENT HOPE THAT WE HAVE THROUGH CHRIST'S VICTORY ACCOMPLISHED IN HIS INCARNATION, ATONING DEATH AND RESURRECTION. THE SURE AND CERTAIN ANCHOR OF THE SOUL, THIS HOPE HAS GIVEN GLADNESS AND ASSURANCE TO FAITHFUL BELIEVERS ALL THROUGHOUT THE CENTURIES OF THE CHURCH'S STRUGGLE WITH THE FORCES OF ENTRENCHED EVIL. IT ASSURES US OF PRESENT VICTORY IN OUR PERSONAL LIVES AND CORPORATE MINISTRY, BUT IT ALSO POINTS TO THE FINAL TRIUMPH WHEN EVERY KNEE SHALL BOW AND EVERY TONGUE SHALL CONFESS THAT JESUS CHRIST IS LORD.

Never have we so needed a renewed sense of the hope that we have in Him. We know the power and devastation of sin, and we acknowledge the increasing degradation of our culture. We are Wesleyans, however; and as our theologians have said, the keynote of our theology is not the "pessimism of [fallen] nature" but the "optimism of grace." We therefore call our Movement to the joyous expectation of victory which so motivated our spiritual forebears to claim the American frontier for Jesus Christ. We cannot cower before the darkness, paralyzed by "the encircling gloom" which continually we must confront. "But where sin abounded, grace did much more abound." The same power which brought the Roman Empire to bow before the cross, renewed the Church in the days of the Protestant Reformation, and reshaped the culture in the Wesleyan Revival is also ours as we encounter the moral depravity and sneering secularism of our times. Let us be joyfully faithful, then, creatively relevant and utterly confident that Jesus' victory is our own. With gladness we do the work which He has given us, even as we await the consummation when all the earth shall echo with the song of conquest, "Alleluia! The Lord God Omnipotent reigns!"

The President and the Bible Faculty
of God's Bible School and College

Chapter 1

A CALL TO BIBLICAL FIDELITY

We affirm that the Holy Scriptures, as the inspired and inerrant Word of God, are the basis of authority in the Church, normative for all our faith and practice.

We call for renewed submission to the absolute authority of the Bible, not as a revered icon, but as the touchstone for both our personal lives and our public proclamation.

TOUCHSTONE FOR EVERYTHING

by Larry D. Smith

It wasn't incense from Heaven that drifted through Brother Gleason's old brick church during Sunday worship. Granted, the saints assembled there did sniff an odor so pungent that for a moment it seemed to take their breath away. However, this wasn't from a censer swung by unseen angels, but from certain of the brothers and sisters who were in need of soap, deodorant and shampoo. Their immortal souls may have been cleansed from pollution, as they probably professed, but their mortal bodies—well, that was another matter!

As a faithful pastor, Brother Gleason was determined to lead his odiferous parishioners to repentance and reform, which in this case meant the scrubbing brush and the sudsy bath. So he stood up in his pulpit one Sabbath day to wage war on dirt, which he denounced as one of the foulest of the devil's works. Emphatically he announced his text, "Cleanliness is next to godliness"—a text that he knew was in the Bible, as he told his congregation, though he could not find it anywhere!*

Years have passed, but as I recall, Brother Gleason's homily produced neither repentance nor reform. His odiferous parishioners, alas, remained his odiferous parishioners. This much is sure—his "sermon" was no sermon at all, for it was based in the instruction of a secular proverb, not in application of Holy Scripture. And that, of course, is what a sermon is supposed to be.

What is worse, his mistaken claim to Biblical authority reflects a serious problem widespread among us—one of several addressed in the "Call to the Conservative Holiness Movement." In addition to its introduction, this document consists of ten sections—ten specific "calls" to recovery and reform.

Its first section, published in this issue, is a "Call to Biblical Fidelity." This is basic to all our faith and practice, for it is an earnest appeal to be ruthlessly honest and utterly faithful to what the Bible really says. It's true that we've always lifted up the Holy Writ with profound honor and respect. *But this is not enough, for we must also shape our purpose to its teaching, not shape its teaching to our purpose.* This is why the first "Call" summons us to "renewed submission to the absolute authority of the Bible, not as a revered icon, but as the touchstone for both our personal lives and our public proclamation."

Remember that church history is punctuated by many "calls" such as this, all pleading for course correction in the life and witness of the Church. They have differed in both attitude and motivation. We mean ours to be humble and respectful, issued in sincere hope that our dear brothers and sisters throughout the Movement will give careful consideration to the proposals that we submit. We love the Wesleyan/Holiness Movement, especially its conservative wing, labeled the CHM, for this is our tiny plot within the Universal Church and our spiritual home in which we gladly live out our lives. This is why we are impelled to "speak the truth in love," convinced as we are, that the CHM stands at a historic crossroads.

In each of our ten specific "calls" we follow a simple pattern, often used in such appeals. This pattern is as follows: *(1) Principle Declared (2) Failure Acknowledged,* and

(3) Correction Offered. With this in mind, we turn now for a closer look at the "Call to Biblical Fidelity."

I. PRINCIPLE DECLARED: *Holy Scripture—Inspired Guide for Salvation*

"As Wesleyans we affirm that the Holy Scriptures as the inspired and inerrant Word of God, are the basis of authority in the Church, normative for all our faith and practice." In these words, the "Call" affirms what we all confess the divine inspiration, absolute truthfulness and binding authority of the Bible—"God's Word written," as a familiar phrase describes it. Like John Wesley, who declared himself "a man of one book," we love the Bible and pay homage to its message.

But the "Call to Biblical Fidelity" also focuses on what is the real issue among us—the actual application of Holy Scripture both to doctrine and discipline as they are enforced in the Church. This is why it quotes the sixth of the *Thirty-Nine Articles of Religion* (issued during the 16th-century Reformation by Anglican divines and later included in American Methodism's unalterable standards of belief) which of course are the legacy of all the Holiness Movement. "Holy Scripture contains everything that is necessary for salvation," as a slightly updated version of the statement declares, adding that no one can be required to believe or do anything "as necessary to salvation" unless it can be proved by the Bible.

II. FAILURE ACKNOWLEDGED: *Holy Scripture—Misapplication of Its Content*

As Methodists, we were formed specifically "to raise up a holy people," acting as a vigorous reform Movement within the broader Church. This is still our mission, and if ever we forget it, we will have no reason even to exist as a distinctive Movement. So it is devastating when "holiness" churches—whether Nazarene, Pilgrim Holiness or Bible Methodist—are no different in piety or purpose from other evangelical congregations scattered across our communities. Yet reform Movements tend to become lopsided in emphasis and read into Scripture what it does not really say.

Thus, as the "Call" acknowledges, "we have often focused on issues and made demands which we cannot legitimately establish from the Holy Scriptures." As we know, the CHM was established largely in protest against "worldliness" and "drift" in the larger Movement. Many aspects of that protest were legitimate, and subsequent history in great measure has justified it. Thank God for the sane, balanced leaders who voiced that protest in clear, positive and winsome tones.

Yet too many of us were carried into extremes, sometimes misapplying Scripture, giving it application which legitimate exegesis did not suggest nor validate. From our pulpits and publications came "trivial notions and speculations," as the "Call" describes them; and sometimes these became the expected lifestyle "standards" in our churches. There are pockets in the CHM where this is still true.

Some of the polarization in our Movement today can be traced to understandable reaction to these excesses. Granted, we are now facing our own crisis with "worldliness and drift," fueled too often by affluent lifestyles and rebellion against legitimate interpretations of the Bible's call to separated living. But this is not the only reason for our problems. To some extent, we are reaping a bitter harvest from earlier misapplications of Holy Scripture and consequent extremes.

III. CORRECTION OFFERED: *Holy Scripture—Touchstone for Faith and Practice*

"Stand humbly and quietly before the Book," advised Dr. William Sangster. *"Let its great truths soak in. Through the operation of the Holy Spirit it will search your soul, expose the shams and deceits, reveal the truth of God to you, and bring you to the Cross."* This is what the "Call to Biblical Fidelity" is saying in its appeal for submission to "the absolute authority of the Bible, not as a revered icon but as the touchstone for both our personal lives and our public proclamation." An icon is a sacred image or symbol, highly honored but quickly forgotten. In contrast, a touchstone is "a siliceous stone used to test the purity of gold and silver," as the dictionary informs us. This is why the term is now used for a criterion or standard of judgment to determine genuineness or authenticity. That's what the Bible must be to us—"a touchstone" that determines the genuineness of everything.

If this really is to happen, let me suggest that we do the following:

- *Center our preaching in the Word of God.* This must be more than a brief text initially quoted but soon forgotten in a rambling discussion of pious opinions and scattered proof texts. Our pulpits must exegete and apply the Bible.

- *Restore Scripture lessons to public worship.* This ancient practice continues in many denominations. But among us, the Bible is seldom read in church except for the preacher's text. If we're serious about the Bible, we should read it publicly as an act of worship.

- *Catechize our people, and especially our youth.* This means systematic, Bible-based instruction in what we are to believe and how we are to live. Many of our churches have no other means of spiritual formation except trips to the public altar.

- *Center traditional lifestyle standards firmly and fairly in the Scriptures.* In reaction to past excesses, too many of our pastors and teachers are failing to give instruction from the Word on how to live a holy, separated life. We must drop those issues that we cannot prove by Scripture, at least as "necessary to salvation," and preach those that we can. Otherwise we will lose them.

No, it wasn't incense from Heaven that drifted through Brother Gleason's old brick church during Sunday worship. That was neither to be expected nor desired. But the Word of God should have echoed from its walls, carefully explained and faithfully enforced. Whether that would have moved his odiferous saints to the scrubbing brush and the sudsy bath I do not know. But this much is sure: they should have been challenged as we should all be challenged by something more than the instruction of a secular proverb. We must all be confronted by the authority of the Bible—"the touchstone for all our faith and practice."

* This true anecdote was told to the editor by his father, Rev. Dean Smith, although the pastor's name has been changed.

"THE BIBLE SAYS"

by Michael R. Avery

When my boys were very small, I would often give them their "Saturday night bath." This weekly ritual involved a long warm soak, a robust scrubbing and a vigorous shampoo, leaving them squeaky clean. The boys loved the playful soak, tolerated the scrubbing, but became quite agitated when I would reach for the shampoo. It may have had something to do with the fact that I used such copious amounts that rinsing it out of their hair became an experience close to drowning.

One Saturday night, all was going well until I reached for the bottle of shampoo. My older son, who obviously had had enough, stood up in the front of the tub, pointed his finger at me, and with evangelistic fervor shouted, "The Bible says, 'Thou shalt not wash a little boy's hair with shampoo'!" My son had a remarkable grasp of the authority of Scripture, yet at the tender age of three, he had not yet acquired an exact understanding of how to use it—or more accurately how not to use it for his own designs and purposes.

A less than careful use of Scripture is a slippery slope for both men and Movements. Most religious traditions, including our own Conservative Holiness Movement, have not escaped this pitfall. As the "Call to the Conservative Holiness Movement" states, "We have often focused on issues and made demands which we cannot legitimately establish from the Scriptures. As a result, trivial notions and speculations at times have marred our witness." The CHM has, for the most part, been comprised by a group of people who have placed a very high value on Scripture. Our willingness to live out many unpopular Biblical values is a testimony to this. However, we have not always had an equally high commitment to the careful exegesis of Scripture, which is crucial to preserving Biblical fidelity.

Webster has defined fidelity as "the quality of being faithful; of accuracy in detail; exactness." The dictionary adds an interesting modern analogy to explain fidelity: "The degree to which an electronic device (as a record player or radio) accurately reproduces the original sound." With this in mind we can define Biblical fidelity.

Biblical fidelity then is to reproduce faithfully and accurately the thoughts, meaning and intent of Scripture in both our preaching and practice.

Every tradition, including the CHM, works in a subculture of its own. These subcultures gravitate toward certain theological, cultural and religious biases that inevitably serve as lenses through which Scripture is viewed and applied to Christian living. For the most part this is healthy and normative. It is not, however, without problems, for all Biblical and theological biases must be held in check by an unyielding commitment to be both honest and faithful to the Scriptural text. If this does not happen, Biblical fidelity is compromised or even lost.

Are there any particular ways the CHM needs to be more careful? Yes. Let me offer a few that I believe are especially applicable to the CHM.

1. The CHM must be careful not to practice eisegesis instead of exegesis.

Eisegesis is an interpretation of Scripture that expresses the interpreter's own views rather than the text's true meaning (*exegesis*). When we impose our own theological, cultural or personal views on a text, despite knowing that faithful scholarship will not support our interpretation, we compromise the truth and fail to honor God's Word. The CHM must regularly remind itself that Scripture is the standard by which we test all other truth claims, not the other way around.

2. **The CHM must be careful not to blur the line between Biblical principle and religious tradition.**

Tradition is a valuable part of our Christian life. Traditions may certainly be taught in our homes and churches, but they should be taught as traditions, not as divine revelation. Traditions must never be confused with God-given commands or given the same authority and weight as Scripture. When this confusion occurs, the end result can be a church that has replaced the authority of God's Word with the deadening weight of traditionalism or, worse, just trivia.

3. **The CHM must be careful not to misinterpret "questions" as "questioning" and inadvertently discourage honesty!**

It is impossible to respect God's Word too highly, but it is possible to respect it wrongly. We must let people know that it is not irreverent to see difficulties in the Biblical text and allow them to think hard and honestly about how these difficulties can be resolved. You have not truly studied the Bible until you have asked hard questions of it. However, in some people's minds "asking hard questions" is the same as "posing problems," and we have been discouraged all our lives from finding problems in the Bible. Let me assure you, the Bible can handle scrutiny. Honesty is a vital part of Biblical fidelity. God would rather have honest disagreement from one committed to His Word than forced affirmation of something we don't really believe or understand.

4. The CHM must be careful not to allow the externalization of Biblical standards to substitute for the internalization of Biblical character.

The Bible was not written to be a curiosity shop from which we pick and choose certain things to obey in our lives like one might pick and choose an article of clothing. Rather, it was written to transform us from the inside out! One can know and honor the Bible in visible ways (especially those that make us look spiritual in our setting), yet fail to demonstrate the character it commands. One can be meticulous, even legalistic, about his tithe and yet fail ever to develop the spirit of generosity. One can dress modestly and still have a sensuous spirit. Sheer knowledge of the Bible doesn't make one godly. The mere application of a few visible commands doesn't mean we have cultivated holy character. One can read the Bible daily, acquire significant amounts of Biblical knowledge, adopt standards of dress and behavior, yet have no straight-line correspondence between that and real Christlikeness.

It would be helpful for all of us to remember that the "sounds" our lives make on earth reach Heaven either as the scratchy, tinny, garbled clanging of carnality or as harmonic, melodious, pleasant reproductions of Christlikeness. Our success at being like Jesus will be determined not only by knowing with a high degree of accuracy what the Bible says but also by honestly living it out.

Chapter 2

A CALL TO HISTORIC ROOTS AND CONTINUITY

We affirm our allegiance to the classical Christianity of the centuries, confessing its faith, sharing its historic witness, living out its godly discipline, and claiming all of its treasures as our own.

We call for a "league offensive and defensive with every soldier of Christ," reclaiming the richness of our Christian heritage and our essential unity with all who truly confess Him as Lord.

SPIRITUAL ROOTS

by Michael R. Avery

No one possesses a faith that is self made. All of us are indebted to the whole body of Christ for our understanding of Scripture and our view of Christian living. We have all benefited immensely from great spiritual truths that have been developed over the centuries, shaped by revival, purified by reformation, and tested by experience. We stand on the shoulders of men and Movements who have forged for us what we now know as our spiritual heritage. To unwittingly sever ourselves from these spiritual roots is tragic. To knowingly do so may well be treacherous. Yet many Christians sell their spiritual birthright as thoughtlessly as they sell their unwanted household junk.

What these yard sale saints can't see is not hidden to historical scholars. They tell us that Movements, religious or otherwise, can only maintain vitality and significance as long as they retain a clear understanding of their historical identity. A religious Movement's identity is determined by its dogma, doctrine, traditions, ideals, values and culture—all of which have been developed over the centuries. These are the things that tell us who we are and answer the question of why we exist. Without them, no Movement can affirm a clear mission or cast a unifying vision.

The "Call to the Conservative Holiness Movement" pleads for a commitment to historic roots and continuity in Article II. This involves both a renewed commitment to classical Christianity and a renewed understanding of our spiritual heritage as passed down to us through the Methodist Holiness tradition. This call is not rooted in a sentimental hankering for the past. Nor is it some nostalgic desire to recreate methods and means that have long since served their usefulness—that's what museums do! It is, however, recognition that we lose something vitally important for our future when we become disconnected from our past.

This appeal to the CHM is particularly urgent for two reasons. First, the CHM is going through a time of transition. Second, the CHM is too often afflicted with a form of historical amnesia; we have long-term memory loss. Our memory only reaches back about 60 years to the days when we separated from our mother churches. What happened then is clearly a vital part of our heritage, but it is far from all of it. Nor can that separation point be the sole place from which we draw our identity. If it is, then we lose the wealth of hundreds of years of rich holiness history. We also lose important "family traits" and "traditions" that may serve us well in our contemporary struggles. The CHM faces questions today and will certainly face more in the tomorrows that will not be adequately answered without drawing on the wisdom and life experiences of our forefathers. We need our heritage—all of it!

As the CHM seeks to develop a fuller understanding of its historical identity, it is helpful to examine the family tree. We are Christian; we are Reformation Protestant; we are Arminian; we are Arminian/Anglican; and we are Methodist. From there the branch divides into Wesleyan Methodist, Free Methodist, Pilgrim Holiness and Nazarene. From there the branches further divide into a dozen denominational groups and a host of independent churches that self identify as the Conservative Holiness Movement.

The CHM is, for the most part, Wesleyan in its theological opinions, especially in its commitment to the doctrine of entire sanctification. However, it can be quite diverse in many other ways. There is significant variation in views relating to the sacraments, lifestyle practices, social issues (e.g. divorce and remarriage) and church government. The CHM does find common ground in its opposition to immodest worldly attire, short hair on women and the wearing of jewelry. These common ground issues have become the "street level" means of identifying the Movement. As important as these things may be, there are some other very important "family traits" that ought to be front and center when people think of the CHM-identity markers that I would love to see become our "street level" means of identity—traits that can clearly be found in our spiritual roots, in particular our Methodist Holiness heritage!

The early Methodists found their reason for existence and their vision for the future in Wesley's call "to reform the nation, and in particular the church, and to spread scriptural holiness over the land." Responding to that call led them to reap a harvest of souls for God's kingdom and ultimately altered the religious landscape of England and early America for almost a century. However, it must be noted that this breathtaking, forward-looking, mission statement worked only in a context. And that context was the theological content and spiritual character of what Methodism truly was. You could call it their DNA or their family traits. Let's examine five of those traits.

First, they were known ***for a distinctive theological understanding of God.*** One of the best ways to understand the impact of their theology is to look at how those early Methodists lived it out. Francis Asbury, the founder of American Methodism, is a good example to observe. When Asbury arrived in America there were only a few hundred Methodists, but by 1860 one out of every three Americans was a Methodist. Asbury crossed the Allegheny Mountains on horseback 60 times, slept in 10,000 different cabins and homes, preached 60,500 sermons in 45 years (a little more than one a day), and became more recognizable than George Washington or Thomas Jefferson. By the end of the 18th century, Methodism had determined the nature of religious culture in America, thus setting the stage for the next 100 years.

Why did he and countless hundreds of other Methodist circuit riders do what they did? It was their theology that motivated them! Their theology taught them that every man had infinite worth. They believed that God not only wanted to save every man but that every man could be saved! To better understand this, you need to remember that Calvinism was the prevalent theology of the day, and a core component of Calvinism was "election." When the average Calvinist walked down the street, he would think, "It is possible that I might even see one of God's elect today." When a Methodist walked down the street, he would think, "Every man I see today can be one of God's elect, and it is my job to tell him!"

Second, they were known for *their optimism of grace.* I am not sure if grace shaped their eschatology, or their eschatology shaped their concept of grace, but what I do know is that the early Methodists believed so powerfully in the transforming grace of God that they were convinced that they would transform the church, the nation, and the world—ushering in the millennial reign! The optimism of grace drove Methodist circuit riders farther and faster than new invention could drive the feet of commerce.

Third, they were known for *a distinctive view of spiritual experience.* The early Methodists believed that every man could be saved, that every man could know he was saved, and that every man could be saved to the uttermost! The doctrine of assurance gave new converts stability and peace. The doctrine of entire sanctification gave believers victory over sin and power to live a holy life. Methodism took people out of their "sinning religion" and taught them that they could walk in complete obedience to God! With such peace, hope, and victory, it's no wonder that the Methodists were known for their exuberant singing and loud shouting!

Fourth, they were known for *their distinctive view of the church and evangelism.* They were flexible and innovative. They didn't need a proper church with stained-glass windows and comfortable pews. They preached in the highways and byways, in fields and near mines, on the frontier and in the city ghettos. They introduced a new style of worship to accommodate the large numbers of unconverted people in their congregations. Worship scholars refer to it as "frontier worship." It is now the primary worship style we still use today. They operated missions for the down-and-outer, cottages for the unwed mothers, orphanages for the destitute, camp meetings for the masses, class meetings for the newly converted, and circuits for rural churches. They founded training schools, colleges and universities. No aspect of their society was left untouched by the gospel. Those early Methodists did whatever was necessary to obey the command to "preach the gospel to every creature."

Fifth, they were known for *their stewardship.* The early Methodists looked right through the world that was around them and saw a Kingdom. It was to that Kingdom, and ultimately to its King, that they gave their solemn allegiance and perfect love. Many freely denied themselves the comforts of home, family and marriage to give their lives in

His service. The rank and file who did build homes and raise up families were so well known for their rejection of this world's values and ostentation that the very name "Methodist" was spoken in derision and scorn by those who loved to parade their fashion and display their wealth. It was not what could be gained in this world but what could be invested in the world to come that motivated these people called Methodists.

These are a few of the "family traits" of a people and a Movement that history says "owned the 19th century"! I see some of these same traits being manifested today in the underground church in China where 20,000 people are converted every day. It has yet to be decided who will own the 21st century, but I believe it will be owned by the people who have looked long enough and deep enough into the past to see how God will work in the future. You can figure it out, too, but you will need to dig deep into your spiritual roots!

FINDING OUR BIRTH CERTIFICATE

by Larry D. Smith

Did you ever run across your Great-Great-Aunt Gertrude—you know, the one who with her trusty musket held off a dozen murderous savages dancing around her burning cabin? Or meet your Great-Great-Grandfather Dean who marched with General Meade, or perhaps it was General Lee, across the bloody fields of Gettysburg?

We're not talking about midnight visits with departed spirits, but about genealogy—the absorbing quest for information about your ancestors. It's like a detective game that Americans love to play, rummaging through courthouse basements and devouring family websites for births, marriages and deaths from generations past. They squeal excitedly to find in Granny's attic a tattered Bible with handwritten records squeezed between Malachi and Matthew or a faded album with bearded patriarchs and their bonneted and bustled wives.

Family research, as we are told, has now surpassed even stamp collecting as our favorite leisure time pursuit. But this is vastly more than an entertaining hobby. For in this time of disconnection and dislocation, it's become a passionate pursuit to recover roots, restore continuity, renew connection and, more significantly, to reclaim identity. In finding our origins, we find ourselves.

What is true of individuals is also true of institutions. This is why the second article of the "Call to the Conservative Holiness Movement" speaks so pointedly and powerfully to us. Its clear-cut summons to "Historic Roots and Continuity" prods us from the paralyzing amnesia that has stripped too many of us of any sense of ennobling Christian heritage and repositions us firmly in that heritage as both the birthright of our past and the promise of our future.

This emphasis is essential for a healthy, relevant, and united CHM, confident in its defining identity, conscious of its originating purpose, and centered in its fulfilling ministry. So we now consider this second "Call," noting again its simple structure, which is as follows: *(1) Principle Declared, (2) Failure Acknowledged, and (3) Correction Offered.*

I. PRINCIPLE DECLARED: *Our Heritage Affirmed*

"We gladly affirm our allegiance to the classical Christianity of the centuries, confessing its faith, sharing its historic witness, living out its godly discipline, and claiming all of its treasures as our own." In these words, the GBS ministerial faculty anchors the CHM in the classic Christian orthodoxy of all the ages and, as heirs of its priceless riches, asserts allegiance to its doctrine and obedience to its discipline. Our claim, then, is that we're not just a ragtag remnant of squabbling schismatics, but another loyal brigade of earnest Christians—convinced Wesleyans, to be sure, but locked arm-in-arm with all the other faithful soldiers in Jesus' army.

This means that we're marching with the saints—yes, with all of them who follow His "blood red banner [that] streams afar" so triumphantly above us. They come from different generations, traditions and denominations; but without exception they are united in devotion to Him and in dedication to "the faith once and for all delivered unto the saints." Note that the "Call" specifically connects us "to the heroic lives of ancient Christians, the faithful witnesses of the Middle Ages, the stalwart testimonies of the Reformers, the Biblical proclamation of the Wesleys, and the earnest piety of the early Holiness Movement."

Thus, as we readily acknowledge, our foundations reach down far deeper than the beginnings of the CHM. We rejoice in all that is noble in those beginnings, and we revere those heroes who shaped our Movement's early witness. But we must place all of this in the great succession of the ages in what is called "The Great Tradition" of historic Christian orthodoxy—its doctrines, its worship, its sacraments, its discipline and its witness. To reconnect ourselves with this is to forge anew our ties to what Christians have believed and taught everywhere from the Church's earliest days. This adds depth and grandeur to our sense of who we really are, and it will also save us from a narrowness that "at best ... [is] lamentable ignorance," as the "Call" reminds us, "and at worst, sectarian bigotry."

II. FAILURE ACKNOWLEDGED: *Our Heritage Neglected*

"But too often we have smugly disconnected ourselves from our Christian past." Everywhere the Bible points to the warning and inspiration provided by sacred history. Recall the Ebenezer stone that Samuel raised to memorialize triumph over the Philistines, the appeals of the prophets to review God's mighty acts and His righteous purpose, the command of Jesus to remember Him in the broken bread and sacred wine. Because God is deeply concerned for history, we should be also.

In its sweeping panorama, Church history confronts us forcibly with the abiding principles that in every age are irreducibly and unalterably Christian. In narrower terms, it confronts us with the unique vision that God committed to the founders of our specific Movement and which they, in turn, have handed on to us. In this way the CHM is introduced to its spiritual DNA that reveals who we really are and why God raised us up at our beginning.

This is like finding our birth certificate—a birth certificate that we have almost lost beneath the debris accumulated throughout the decades. Such tragedy is beyond our comprehension. For it has left us with only the faintest glimmer from the torches of marching saints whom God has given us as mentors and examples. Even the memory of our birthright as Wesleyans has become increasingly faded and remote. We are left as orphans, rootless and confused.

Our many splits have made this even worse, for every one of them has centered us increasingly in the narrow issues of schism and separation. This has moved us even further from the full-orbed witness of historic Christianity and from the magnificent Wesleyan/holiness focus through which we have received that witness. The results are predictable, for "we have become theologically shallow, spiritually weak, and blind to the work of God in the lives of others. We have withdrawn ourselves into protected enclaves, congratulating ourselves on our superiority over other Christians ... and ignoring the continuing work of the Holy Spirit throughout all the universal Church."

III. CORRECTION OFFERED: Our Heritage Reclaimed

"We call, therefore, with John Wesley, for a 'league offensive and defensive with every soldier of Christ,' reclaiming the richness of our Christian heritage and our essential unity with all who truly confess Him as Lord."

In these words, the "Call to Historic Roots and Continuity" comes to its conclusion, urging us to find our birth certificate and examine it once again. This should cause us, first, to reclaim our heritage in the magnificent Christian orthodoxy shared so gladly by all who confess the name of Jesus and to reaffirm its evangelical conviction that so firmly undergirds its faith and practice. It's all the more imperative now that we unite in a "league offensive and defensive with every soldier of Christ" as we confront the hostile forces of militant secularism determined to destroy every remnant of Christian culture.

But our birth certificate should also renew our loyalty to the foundational principles that shaped our Methodist beginnings and later the formation of the American Holiness Movement and the CHM. Remember that God brought us into being as a reform Movement within the Church—an "evangelical order," as Albert Outler has reminded us, focused in an impassioned mission "to spread scriptural holiness over these lands." Loyalty to the Church Universal is not diminished but enhanced by loyalty to the specific subculture within it that is our immediate spiritual home. Our subculture is the CHM, which we love; and we are called, as were our ancestors, not to attack or rend the broader Church but to call it back to its own original message of holiness of heart and life.

At the same time that we deliberately reconnect with the Great Tradition of Christ's one holy Church, we also deliberately reconnect with the rich insights of our Methodist heritage. The latter enriches and strengthens the former, and the former provides context and catholicity to the latter. From the Wesleys on down through the generations, we hail our own "endless line of splendor"—saints and scholars, missionaries and evangelists, hymn writers, and reformers, lay and clergy—who have heroically and graciously lived out their lives in that pursuit.

Our birthright, therefore, demands vigorous and gracious faithfulness to our heritage as Christians of Wesleyan tradition. But this is not the same as a sterile antiquarianism, which is an unhealthy fixation with ancient relics shaped in futile purpose to "preserve our heritage" as a sort of pickled corpse, propped up for public display but still lifeless and corrupting. Nothing could be more deadly to spiritual life than this—nothing, that is, except the opposite extreme, which is the arrogant rejection of our heritage, forgetting its lessons, ignoring its saints, and scorning its treasures. To idolize the past is to strip our future of its promise; to betray the past is to strip our future of its purpose.

Finding Great-Great-Aunt Gertrude has become a passionate pursuit to recover roots, restore continuity, renew connection and reclaim identity. This is also true of institutions, and that is why the second appeal of the "Call to the Conservative Holiness Movement" speaks so powerfully to us. For it prods us from the paralyzing amnesia that has stripped us of any deep sense of ennobling Christian heritage and repositions us firmly in that heritage as both the birthright of our past and the promise of our future. It's time to find our birth certificate!

Chapter 3

A CALL TO CHRISTIAN COMMUNITY

We affirm the traditional Protestant insistence that the visible Church is the congregation of the faithful in which the "pure Word of God is preached and the sacraments duly administered according to Christ's ordinance."

We call for renewed understanding of the Biblical doctrine of the Church as "the pillar and ground of the truth," reverence for its orthodox confessions, submission to its holy discipline, and faithfulness to its common life.

AS AN ARMY WITH BANNERS

by Larry D. Smith

Open your hymnbook to "Onward, Christian Solders!" Ponder the message of that blazing old war song as its imagery rouses your heart to valor. Let your eyes fall on verse three, then hum the words: *"Like a mighty army / Moves the Church of God, / Brothers, we are treading / Where the saints have trod!"* Ah, yes, you remember—the Church Militant!

Here are Jesus' marching millions who everywhere engage His enemies in bloody combat, as under His command they advance to the final conquest. Their way is marked by the footprints of that heroic vanguard who have forged ahead, the faithful ones above who beckon the faithful ones below to press on until they too have arrived in the Church Triumphant.

Behold, then, Christ's holy Church: the *ekklesia,* His "called out ones," united with Him and one another in "the communion of saints," which is His mystical body and His bride. He has built it foursquare upon Himself, the Rock of our salvation; and as He has promised "the gates of hell shall not prevail against it" (Matt. 16:18).

In brief but vivid words, C.S. Lewis pictures the majestic splendor of this mighty host, "spread out through all time and space and rooted in eternity, terrible as an army with banners." Let this vast panorama take your breath away—Christ's universal Church, holy and everlasting, transcending Heaven and earth, the home of millions here and millions there, the invincible legions of God, claiming all creation for His dominion.

Charles Colson reinforces all this, emphasizing that the Church is "not incidental to the great cosmic struggle for the hearts and souls of modern men and women. It is the instrument which God has chosen for that battle. To bring hope and truth to a needy world, the Church must be the Church!" For as we have said, the Church is Christ's body, "and in that body lives fully the One who fills the whole wide universe" (Eph. 1:23, J.B. Phillips). Christ acts in the world through the Church in which He dwells. This lofty view of the Church, so clearly taught in Scripture, is basic to Article III of the "Call to the Conservative Holiness Movement." Please consider its urgent plea for "Christian Community," noting three areas implicit in its structure: *(1) Principle Declared, (2) Failure Acknowledged, and (3) Correction Offered.*

I. PRINCIPLE DECLARED: *The Church Beloved*

"Union with Christ establishes membership in His Church, the community of the faithful, in all times and places." Life in God means life within the Church, not outside it; for ordinarily, at least, without the Church there is no Christianity at all. For never can the Head be without the body, nor the body without the Head. Neither can we love the Head unless we love the body also, as did Our Lord who so loved the Church that He laid down His life for it (Eph. 5:25).

Its divine functions touch every aspect of our lives. As *a temple*, it offers unceasing worship to the Triune God. As "*the pillar and ground of the truth*" (I Tim. 3:15), it is the repository, guardian and witness to the apostolic faith. As a *kindly mother*, it instructs the young, nourishes the faithful, heals the wounded, raises the fallen and comforts the dying.

As "*salt and light*," the Church calls all creation to submit to God's holy law and receive His holy love. As *a missionary thrust*, it seeks to disciple all the nations, "baptizing them in the name of the Father, and of the Son, and of the Holy Ghost, teaching them to observe all things whatsoever I have commanded you" (Matt. 28:19, 20).

Though expressed in thousands of local congregations and divided into many denominations, the Church is one, embracing all who truly love Our Lord. Though its visible manifestation is distressed by error and marred by false professors, it still is holy, for its Head is holy, as are all of its true and living members. Moreover, the Church is "catholic" or universal, reaching out to everyone in every place, lifting up the whole truth necessary to our salvation. Finally it is apostolic, continually proclaiming Christ crucified and risen from the dead, as did Jesus' first disciples. All this is why the ancient Christians believed that "no one can have God for his father who does not have the Church for his mother."

II. FAILURE ACKNOWLEDGED: *The Church Neglected*

But many holiness people, like other evangelicals, have lost any real sense of connection to anything beyond themselves, their own immediate circle, and perhaps the "Movement" with which they identify. In the CHM, indeed, many of us show minimal allegiance even to our own structures such as our denominations and local congregations. Church membership is not highly prized, nor is submission to godly disciplinary authority. Many of us have become freelance Christians with little sense of the Church, its traditions, its functions or its authority.

For as A.W. Tozer has observed, "Our spiritual philosophy has become warped, our sense of belonging has gone from us, we recognize no authority, obey no rules, take no vows, and are almost altogether undisciplined and feel no sense of loyalty."

Obviously, this is not true for all of us, for some of the most faithful and winsome supporters of the Church in both its local and universal aspects are in the CHM. Still our problem remains as tragic as it is widespread. It is tied to several factors, as we believe—some of which are causes, some of which are effects, and some of which are both.

- ***Individualism.*** We've so emphasized "personal relationship with just me and Jesus" that we've often forgotten that this relationship must be lived out within the life of His Church. Besides, contemporary culture, both secular and religious, emphasizes self-assertion and personal entitlement, both of which militate against any sense of covenanted responsibility.

- ***Distrust.*** Commitment to our own "distinctives" has often developed into harsh judgmentalism against anyone who does not share all of these. This extends to Christians outside the CHM, to be sure; but it also mars our own fellowship with antagonism and distrust. As our critics point out, this mindset is often associated with sectarianism, sterility and shrinkage.

- ***Schism.*** The CHM has been shattered by many separations. Some have been necessary, but many have not. Our broken relationships are a matter of profound distress, for they all witness against the unity of the Church. Mr. Wesley's sermon "On Schism" should be required reading for us all.

- ***Narrowness.*** We began as a reform Movement, called of God to "spread scriptural holiness over these lands." At first this was within the framework of historic, institutional Christianity; but later, as we moved into our own "separated" structures, we tended to focus on our own immediate issues and forget the broader spectrum of the Church's teaching and practice. Witness our neglect of the sacraments. Every division has moved us further away from the fullness of orthodox Christian faith and practice. This removal from the "larger, more 'catholic' context" has been "a prescription for insularity, provincialism, and unfortunately, decline," as Dr. Kenneth Collins has warned.

- ***Loss.*** Our young people and our converts cannot survive outside the warm and loving matrix of the Church which is to nourish them in Christ. But our failure to provide structures for their catechetical instruction and spiritual formation has often left them spiritually motherless and without direction.

III. CORRECTION OFFERED: *The Church Reclaimed*

"We call, therefore, for a renewed understanding of the doctrine of the Church ... reverence for its historic confessions, submission to its holy discipline, and faithfulness to its common life."

In these emphatic words, Article III calls us to recover a profound sense of the Church's scriptural role in our personal and corporate lives. We are specifically directed to these specific areas:

- ***Doctrinal Confession.*** Respect for the Church means "reverence for its historic confessions," the great Christian creeds of antiquity that bear witness to the soaring Trinitarian faith "once and for all delivered to the saints." This means Biblical preaching and instruction with depth and content, for we must teach the Faith to our people.

- ***Godly Submission.*** We're not used to having anyone tell us what to do, but Scripture requires Christians to "obey them that have the rule over you" (Heb. 13:17). Church discipline is required in the New Testament, and it demands informed accountability to Biblical standards of belief and conduct enforced lovingly but faithfully by the Church's leadership.
- ***Consistent Faithfulness.*** We are to live and die within the fellowship of the Church, sharing its joys and sorrows, participating in its worship, and submitting to its guidance. This means love and loyalty, first to our own local congregation, lavishing upon it our fidelity and support; and second to the Church Universal, embracing its holy Faith, guarding its sacred treasures, and affirming its true members.

Behold Christ's Church, "spread out through all time and place and rooted in eternity, terrible as an army with banners!" As we insist, the CHM must reassert its place in this vast panorama, a tiny but loyal legion among Jesus' marching millions, faithful still to its original call "to spread scriptural holiness" everywhere. This precious gift we humbly offer to all our brothers and sisters, even as we humbly receive the gifts they offer us. So we hum the rest of verse three: *"We are not divided; / All one body we; / One in hope and doctrine, / One in charity."*

THE CHURCH – COMMUNITY OF FAITH

by Michael R. Avery

America is blessed with a lot of churches. Some sit astride prominent street corners proudly displaying their architectural glory while others are tucked away indiscreetly between a used-shoe store and a day-old bakery in a weary strip mall on the tired side of town. Some have one-word names like "Grace." Others have names so long that you can't say the full name without stopping to breathe. Most have the stereotypical church look, while others resemble something between a cinema and a warehouse. It is not, however, the architecture they display, the appellation they wear, or the affiliations they boast that makes them a church.

The New Testament doesn't provide a simple concise definition of the Church other than what is found in the meaning of the Greek word for Church (*ekklesia*) which is the "called out ones." What it does provide is long narratives portraying the Church in action, colorful word pictures of what the Church is like, specific duties that the Church should fulfill, doctrinal standards that the Church should teach, and prophetic insights of how the Church can stray from the path and lose its way.

History has taught us that the Church needs periods of reformation and times of revival to keep it doctrinally sound, morally pure and faithful to its calling. At other times, the Church needs change that is less radical and might be described as a course correction. These internal corrections need to be made because the Church has a hard time keeping its balance. Certain imbalances can be attributed to the peculiarities of leadership. Others are derived from simply overemphasizing one truth to the neglect of other balancing truths. The worst imbalances, however, grow out of the fertile soil of fear. When the Church and its leaders do what they do or fail to do what they should do out of fear, the Church will inevitably suffer from some imbalance.

The "Call to the Conservative Holiness Movement," by its very nature, is a challenge to the CHM to address particular areas of weakness or failure. The "Call" is not designed to enumerate all the good things that could be said about the CHM. Article III of the "Call" speaks to the CHM's community of faith and addresses some of the imbalances in the way the CHM views its own community of faith and the community of faith at large. I think it is important to note that even though these imbalances are real and need to be addressed, the average conservative holiness church is a wonderful place to worship. In my opinion, such churches still offer some of the best environments available in which to raise a family, hear the Word of God fearlessly proclaimed, and feel conviction for sin while at the same time finding the power of grace, hearing fervent praying, sensing the moving of God's Spirit, worshiping with people who are serious about everyday holiness, and finding an environment that truly helps one to keep his feet on the narrow path that leads to life eternal!

Nevertheless, the CHM does have a significant imbalance in the way it views its own differing communities of faith as well as how it views the larger community of faith. The Movement at large and the various denominations within it suffer from a culture of suspicion toward those who do not share their peculiarities. They also suffer from a certain insularity that robs them of the insight, wisdom and balance that could be derived from the larger Christian community. This condition varies in degree from denomination to denomination and from church to church, but it is present and needs to be honestly confronted and openly addressed.

A CULTURE OF SUSPICION

The CHM highly values the Biblical call to separation from the world. As appropriate and good as this may be, inherent in any serious commitment to "Biblical separation" is the temptation to be suspicious of others who may have a lesser degree or even a greater degree of separation than we do. Just as the call to holy living can veer off the path into perfectionism, the call to separation from the world can veer off the path into isolationism—an isolation that breeds a carnal suspicion of anyone and everyone who doesn't "see it like I do" or share my particular version of how the faithful ought to manifest their faith. This has been a perennial bane for the CHM. Rev. Tom Reed says this kind of suspicion has caused us to "play God—determining who is or is not a Christian based on the way we see things."

Clearly if this suspicion is left unchecked, it will lead to a spirit of judging and condemnation of the larger community of faith, as well as to divisions within our own CHM family. Even now many groups within the CHM will not use a speaker from another group within the CHM because of suspicion and fear. Conservative leaders could use their influence and voice to help remedy this disease with a cure that doesn't require anyone to compromise his corporate values or personal convictions. It only requires a renewed understanding and commitment to the teachings of I Corinthians 8-10 and Romans 14. Add to that a fresh supply of the *"love of God poured out in our hearts by the Holy Spirit,"* and we can be well on our way to removing the ethos of suspicion and division among us.

A DETACHMENT FROM THE LARGER CHRISTIAN COMMUNITY

In I Corinthians 12, Paul reminds us that the Church is a body made up of many different members, each contributing something that the other members cannot give. This has an application to both the local body and to the larger body of Christ. It seems to me that God has given the various traditions of the Christian Church particular insights into truth and practice that He has not given in the same degree to all. He must expect us to learn from one another. I have learned much about prayer by reading from both Catholic and evangelical writers.

I have been immeasurably enriched by the writings and teachings of evangelicals like C.S. Lewis, Dallas Willard, Richard Foster, Ravi Zacharias and Chuck Colson. The expository preaching and teaching of men like John MacArthur, David Jeremiah and Howard Hendricks have added great value to the life of the whole Church and challenged others to take the Scriptures more seriously. The work of William Booth, Mother Teresa and Erlo Stegen have challenged me to the core of my spiritual being to be mindful of the downtrodden and disenfranchised among us. Where would America's families be today without the ministry of James Dobson? Personally, no one has challenged me more in the area of spiritual intimacy and holiness than Dennis Kinlaw and John Oswalt.

It must be noted that not a single name mentioned above identifies with the CHM. Yet each one of them has spoken powerfully to my life and the lives of many conservative holiness people. In preparation for writing this article, I spoke with Rev. Tom Reed, who is an elder statesman within the CHM. He shared with me a list of men outside our tradition who have been used of God to advance his own spiritual life. He mentioned H.A. Ironsides (a former pastor of Moody church), A.W. Tozer (he visited his church often on Sunday evenings), Paul Rees, Vance Havner, S.M. Lockridge, and Howard Hendricks. He added this insightful comment, "These were not *holiness* men, but they were *holy* men, and I refuse to write them off just because they see some things differently than I do."

Those in the CHM have tended to isolate themselves from these "outside" voices. They fear that they might be a corruptive or a persuasive influence, or even worse, that if we allow anyone to minister to us who does not fully share all our values, we have somehow compromised and demeaned those values. Some of this kind of thinking grows out of simple fear. In other cases I think it is because we have failed to distinguish between a "Romans 14" category issue (opinions, preferences, interpretations, etc.) and a "Galatians 1" category issue (false doctrine or heresy) and have treated all outside voices as if they were in the Galatians 1 category. Mature leaders should be more discerning than this. I know many laymen who already exercise this kind of discernment by means of radio, books, CD's and DVD's that they buy and listen to.

Let me be clear. I am not advocating an open door policy on "outside voices." I am certainly not encouraging local churches to open up their pulpits to men and women from other traditions. What I am suggesting is that in our large conventions, conferences and forums we need occasionally to hear what our brothers and sisters outside the CHM have to say to us. God is working powerfully in His world through many of these choice servants. There are many outside our little circle who are far outstripping us in their passion for the lost, their zeal for the disenfranchised, their insight into Scripture, and their love for holiness. To hear what they are doing, to be challenged by their successes, and to learn from their insight will not and does not diminish my love for my Zion nor make me want to jettison my spiritual tradition and values! It simply makes me a better servant of the Lord!

WE HAVE SOMETHING TO OFFER THE CHURCH

The sword of isolation cuts two ways. We are cut off from what the larger Christian community can give us, and the larger Christian community is cut off from what we can bring to it. The CHM is the beneficiary of hundreds of years of rich holiness heritage. We have grown up embracing and experiencing truths that some in the body of Christ will never know or experience. We have some preachers who are as capable and anointed as any out there anywhere. Our emphasis on personal transformation, purity of heart, perfect love, real character development, growth in grace and freedom from the power of sin are emphases that are needed by the larger body of Christ! Surely what God has freely bestowed on us we ought to freely share with others!

My plea is not for some silly, stupid ecumenicalism! It is a simple plea for us to both reap and share the bounty of spiritual riches that are ours in Christ and found within the various members of His Body, including our own. The late H.E. Schmul, one of the greatest conservative holiness statesmen I ever knew, used to lead us in singing, *"I don't care what church you belong to / Just as long as for Calvary you stand / Just as long as your heart beats with my heart / You're my brother, so give me your hand."* Somebody strike the tune, and let's sing it again!

Chapter 4

A CALL TO CHRISTIAN HOLINESS

We call our Movement to a renewed love for God from which will blossom consistent and winsome lives of holiness, first in motivating purpose, and second in outward conduct.

There is a certain amount of tension and balance in which every Biblical truth must be held. The same is certainly true of the call to holiness. The balance wheel for holiness is unadulterated love for God and others. If holiness loses that balance, it will become a crotchety, sterile, loveless way of rules and regulations that values law over love.

HOLINESS

by Michael R. Avery

I was sitting in the barber's chair when my barber, Tony, asked me what I was working on that day. I told him I was writing. He asked me what I was writing about. I told him I was writing on the subject of "holiness." He grew very quiet and finally said, "That's a subject nobody talks about. Of all the things that get talked about in here, I have never heard anybody talk about holiness."

Tony is right. Holiness is certainly not in the top ten lists of today's societal values. The media will only talk about it when they have the opportunity to mock a morally decent person as a hypocrite; otherwise, the subject is just too boring. Movies typically cast the morally upright as some "out of touch simpleton" whose attempts to do the right thing are valued only for a few laughs. Sadly, most people have never heard a sound, scriptural discussion on holy living—not even in church.

The subject of holiness desperately needs to be rediscovered and reintroduced into the culture and values of America. That process should begin in the church. The practical presentation of holiness has long since been cast out of the pulpits and publishing houses of the people who once made it a household word in America—the Methodists. Actually, many of the 20th century holiness groups, who are the spiritual descendants of early Methodism, have also de-emphasized the message or abandoned it altogether in their quest for respectability and acceptance at the table with mainstream evangelicals.

It is true that evangelicalism has become the dominant expression of Christianity in America. But it is also true that the moral and spiritual life of the nation has collapsed while embracing its flimsy offers of cheap grace, the promise of Heaven no matter how you live, and the disgusting doctrinal conclusions that Christians are just "*saved sinners*" who are far from "*perfect*" but are "*forgiven*" nonetheless. It shouldn't surprise any of us when surveys show that there is almost no difference at all in the core values between the churched and the unchurched in America! What is missing? Holiness!

The Biblical call to holiness leaves no room for Christians who want to coddle sin and live in a state of perpetual immaturity and worldliness. Not only does scriptural holiness teach that Christians can be liberated from willful sin and empowered to live lives of obedience to Christ, but it also teaches that the Christian can be cleansed from the inner propensity to rebellion, selfishness and pride through the work of the Holy Spirit. A holy life is a life where spiritual and moral character is taking root and being lived out in a sensible, upright and godly way.

This is the message that birthed the Wesleyan Revival, took 19th century America by storm and raised the level of social and moral concern on two continents! The post-Civil War holiness revival impacted numerous denominations in America and influenced many Christian leaders outside the Methodist holiness tradition.

Oswald Chambers, a Scottish Baptist, for example, was significantly affected both spiritually and theologically by his association with the American Holiness Movement. In his popular devotional *My Utmost for His Highest*, he wrote, "Continually restate to yourself what the purpose of your life is. The destined end of man is not happiness, nor health, but holiness. … God has one destined end for mankind, viz., holiness. Never tolerate through sympathy with yourself or with others any practice that is not in keeping with a holy God. Holiness means unsullied walking with the feet, unsullied talking with the tongue, unsullied thinking with the mind—every detail of the life under the scrutiny of God."

Many in the broader holiness Movement today would be embarrassed by Chambers' words. They would see them as extreme, maybe even hypocritical. However, there is still a clear witness to the historic message of scriptural holiness! The Francis Asbury Society is a strong voice among Methodists. The mainline holiness groups still have a few scholars, pastors and laity who aren't ashamed to lift the torch for scriptural holiness.

The most welcoming home for the holiness message is among the Conservative Holiness Movement. Members of the CHM write it in their church disciplines, teach it in their Bible colleges, preach it in their pulpits, editorialize it in their periodicals, celebrate it in their testimonies, and emphasize it in their conventions. For the most part, the CHM is strongly committed to the message of holiness.

However, providing the message of scriptural holiness a home and keeping it healthy are not one and the same. The "Call to the Conservative Holiness Movement" addresses this in Article IV. The "Call" points out certain weaknesses that can and will undermine the message. Let me enumerate some of my own concerns with the CHM's stewardship of the holiness message.

I am concerned about legalism. That scriptural holiness has behavioral and lifestyle ramifications cannot be argued; external matters are not unimportant. But when we turn our primary focus away from the heart and onto externals (usually particular standards of dress or modes of behavior), we are in danger of reducing holy virtue to custom and thereby trivializing both.

I am concerned about "works righteousness." Holiness people take the formation of moral and spiritual character seriously. However, the balance between God's work in us and our work in forming holy habits can be threatened more easily than one might think. God graciously invites us to work in cooperation with the Holy Spirit through a variety of spiritual disciplines appropriate to our need, but it is always God at work in us. We have nothing that has not been given to us by the Holy Spirit.

All holiness is God's holiness in us! The temptation to believe that any progress forward is somehow our own doing can be a very real problem. The tendency to believe that careful obedience to Biblical principles or personal adherence to codes or cultures of lifestyle somehow earns merit or standing with God is a subtle form of pride that must be rooted out. Andrew Murray reminds us, "There is no pride so dangerous, none so subtle and insidious, as the pride of holiness." Deep devotion to Christ and careful attention to righteous living must be motivated by loving obedience, or we will fall into the ditch of works righteousness.

I am concerned about perfectionism. Holy people have not attained a state of "sinless perfection" that renders them incapable of any wrong action. Holiness involves both purity and maturity. There is still much room for growth in the sanctified life. Holy habits deepen into fixed patterns of living as we learn to walk in the Spirit. We can and do make many mistakes. There may be times when our attitudes or actions are simply wrong. When that happens we should, in good old honest humility, exercise repentance, make amends and learn from our failures. We never learn from failures denied. Only by seeing them, admitting them and mending them in total meekness will we follow Peter's admonition to "grow in grace and in the knowledge of our Lord and Savior Jesus Christ" (II Peter 3:18).

This is how holy people respond to failure. However, perfectionism cuts us off from our essential humanity, forcing us to deny who and what we really are, or to downplay or outright deny what we have done. When this happens we are simply pretending we are something we are not, and such duplicitous behavior is destructive. True holiness is not the breeding ground for pretentious behavior or self-righteousness. Rather it is the womb in which honesty and humility are nurtured.

I am concerned about message drift. There is a certain amount of tension and balance in which every Biblical truth must be held. The same is certainly true of the call to holiness. The balance wheel for holiness is unadulterated love for God and others. If holiness loses that balance, it will become a crotchety, sterile, loveless way of rules and regulations that values law over love. One ends up behaving like the priest who valued unsullied hands for temple service more than helping the wounded Samaritan out of the ditch. It can also go the other direction and become nothing more than a mental ascent to a positional sanctification that is void of any real sanctity. The theological concept of being "in Christ" is reduced to nothing more than a convenient semantic cover-up for a life of sin and failure. I fear both extremes. Scriptural holiness will not take you down either path.

I am concerned about isolation. The CHM has made valiant attempts to honor the Biblical call to separation from the world, but in doing so it has simply become isolated from the world, thereby hiding its candle under a bushel. The message of holiness needs to be lived out loudly in the marketplace of life, and we are the people to do it! It needs to be broadcast over the Web, printed in books, and argued as the path to true happiness for individuals and families.

My barber is right. You don't hear talk about holiness in the barber shops, bakeries or board rooms of America. But the day will come when "Holiness unto the Lord" will resound throughout the earth and be part of an eternal conversation by those who have pursued that "holiness without which no man shall see the Lord." I want to be one who promotes the conversation now, don't you?

HOLINESS: BEYOND THE SLOGANS!

by Larry D. Smith

"Holiness!" Here's a word that will bring the house down at camp meetings all across America. Just let the evangelist slap the pulpit, announcing, "Holiness is why we're having this meeting tonight!" Often there will be a chorus of amens so vibrant that it will seem to bounce off the rafters and rise up to Heaven itself.

This is fitting, of course, for what the evangelist says is right. Holiness is basic to every act of Christian worship, whether it's in a rude country tabernacle or an elegant city church. But that's not all, for holiness is also basic to every other act of Christian life. That's why we repeat Hebrews 12:14 so often: "Follow peace with all men, and holiness, without which no man shall see the Lord."

So it's for the best of reasons that we're the Conservative *Holiness* Movement, founded to keep alive the passion that gave us birth. For until the trumpet sounds we're under divine commission to "spread scriptural holiness" everywhere and thus "to raise up a holy people." For holiness is "religion itself," as John Wesley said, for it's all about being authentic followers of Jesus.

This is why Article IV of the "Call to the Conservative Holiness Movement" is so emphatic: *"Holiness of heart and life flowing out of love for God, as we believe, is the 'central idea of Christianity,' for this is God's redemptive purpose for our fallen humanity."* Let us now examine what else the "Call" asserts about this "central idea" (the term was first used by Bishop Peck) and its present relationship to our Movement.

I. PRINCIPLE DECLARED: *The Holiness Witness Affirmed*

"Be ye holy for I am holy" (I Pet. 1:16). But what does this really mean? Dr. W.T. Purkiser answers that in Biblical usage, holiness embraces the concepts of *"separation from the profane and unholy and devotement to God,"* stressed in the Old Testament, and *"moral purity,"* predominant in the New Testament. Thus, the basic meaning is "separated, consecrated and/or purified; made free from sin."

Separated, consecrated, purified. Yes, these terms define holiness as we have preached it from the days of the Methodist Revival. They point firmly to what is essential to all authentic relationships with God, ensuring that both our outward acts and our inward motives be freed from sin and brought into submission to His will and purpose. *"Accordingly as he hath chosen us in Him before the foundation of the world, that we should be holy and without blame before Him in love" (Eph. 1:4).*

Only God can transform us sinners into saints, freeing us from ingrained selfishness and enabling us to love Him with all our heart, soul, mind and strength and our neighbors as ourselves, as He enjoins. This is the sanctifying work of the Spirit, renewing our fallen nature as He implants His life in us, the life of love, forming all Christ-like graces and expelling all sinful barriers that impede them. Thus in breathtaking splendor we become "partakers of the divine nature"; human and fallible yet, to be sure, but even now, "holy and without blame before him in love."

In conversion, He initially sanctifies us; in expanding development, He progressively sanctifies us; and in perfected love, He entirely sanctifies us. But although sanctification is entirely His gift, it also must be entirely our pursuit; and in the dynamic of grace, the more we seek for holiness, the more holiness we shall be given. All of this is to enable us to live the "Jesus life"—"transformed into the same image from glory to glory, just as by the Spirit of the Lord" (II Cor. 3:18).

II. FAILURE ACKNOWLEDGED: *The Holiness Witness Weakened*

God be praised for that continuing stream of sane, balanced, scriptural spirituality among us, exemplified by thousands of earnest, happy and consistent Christians whose saintly lives have witnessed to the truth of our central emphasis on holiness of heart and life. Thousands are now in Heaven because of this, and the world below is also a better place because of it.

"We confess, however, that our passion for holiness of heart and life has sometimes been reduced merely to external codes and prohibitions, and 'holier-than-thou' attitudes toward those who differ from us. As such we have become shell without substance and betrayed the Scriptural mandate to be holy, because the Lord our God is holy."

This statement from the "Call," however, acknowledges that distortions have clouded our holiness witness—distortions that we must honestly confront, for they leave us "shell without substance." In religion this is a special peril, for sacred words are often used for their pious sound even when they are stripped of authentic content. Among us, for example, holiness can easily become more of a revival slogan or a sectarian buzzword than it is the gracious, loving life of Jesus winsomely displayed in His saints.

It is with a deep sense of love for the CHM, my spiritual home, that I suggest these areas that have given imbalance to our message:

- ***Externalism.*** Holiness is always ethical. For as the Bible teaches, it is always demonstrated by our pursuit of what is right and our rejection of what is wrong. Our danger is that sometimes we have substituted outward conduct—"external codes and prohibitions," as the "Call" explains, for the "inward principle" set in our hearts by the Spirit. In doing this, we make sanctification a way of works rather than a way of faith. Fussy nitpicking and harsh legalism become more our focus than perfect love graciously lived and winsomely portrayed.
- ***Enculturation.*** This is simply giving in to the degraded values of society around us. Once we put great stress on "separation from the world," sometimes to embarrassing extremes. But generally our problem is now the opposite. Historical drift is all too painfully apparent. Scriptural standards of modesty in dress, reverent observance of the Lord's Day, careful stewardship of money, and conscientious restraint in entertainment are increasingly eroded. Much of this is fueled by embourgeoisement, the rising social mobility that comes with increased prosperity. But remember, true holiness will never flourish in an atmosphere of compromise and worldliness.
- ***Sentimentalism.*** This is a mushy religion of exhilarating "frames and feelings," centered more in personal emotional satisfaction than in holy love for God and people. How desperately we need the old Methodist emphasis on godly character, habituated virtue and covenanted accountability! This is that blessed "Christianity in earnest" that increasingly characterizes close and faithful communion with God. Granted, subjec-

tive emotional response is normative and proper, but it must always be welcomed in the context of objective truth and holy duty. Otherwise we become more fixated on feelings about "traveling on" than we are in doing the works of piety that God commands in our devotion to Him or the works of mercy that He commands in our duties to others.

- ***Sectarianism.*** Too often we've assumed that holiness is mostly the exclusive property of the CHM. As the "Call" declares, this overestimation of ourselves has resulted in ugly "holier-than-thou" attitudes toward Christians who are not members of our own particular tribe among all the tribes of Israel. As we must acknowledge, God has winsomely set forth His grace in the lives of all His dear ones in every part of orthodox Christianity—in the lives of all who earnestly pursue that holiness without which none of us shall see the Lord.

III. CORRECTION OFFERED: *The Holiness Witness Reasserted*

We must be who God has called us to be. This is why the "Call" urges us "to a renewed love for God from which will blossom consistent and winsome lives of holiness, first in motivating purpose, and second, in outward conduct." This certainly implies the following:

- ***Personal Godliness.*** Each of us who pursues the holy way must cultivate in ourselves a profound love for Christ, living the life of faith which is demonstrated in faithful duty and holy tempers, embracing "love, peace, joy, longsuffering, gentleness, goodness, faith, meekness, temperance." We need learned expositions of Christian holiness. But even more, we need holiness illustrated by consistent and attractive examples.

- ***Focused Instruction.*** Sometimes we've been better at calling sinners to repentance than in establishing saints in holiness. To correct this imbalance we must provide sound and scriptural materials, attractively presented, that will establish our people in what true Christian sanctity really means.

- ***Balanced Preaching.*** It's essential that we have Biblical preaching that balances the Law with the Gospel. Once we overdid the first at the expense of the second. Now it's the other way around. Sin with all its horror must be faithfully and specifically denounced; while grace with all its promises must be lovingly and lavishly offered.

- ***Structured Accountability.*** We'll probably never bring back the Methodist class meeting, our historic means of spiritual formation. But somehow we must recapture its sense of covenant commitment and consistent accountability, all within an atmosphere of loving affirmation. Small group ministries to promote authentic piety can still accomplish this.

In conclusion, let us boldly reaffirm our foundational conviction that "the great central pervading idea of the whole Book of God from the beginning to the end," as Dr. John McClintock, that fine old Methodist educator, once declared, is "the holiness of the human soul, heart, mind, and will." This means that we must also share his conviction that "our work is a moral work; that is to say, the work of making men holy ... there is our mission, there is our glory, there is our power, and there shall be the ground of our triumph. God keep us true!"

Amen! God keep us true!

Chapter 5

A CALL TO METHODIST PIETY

We call for our Movement to return to our originating commitment to principled covenant with God, which includes (1) the renunciation of all known sin, (2) the embracing of all positive virtue, and (3) the faithful practice of the means of grace, especially "the instituted means of grace," defined as the Word, prayer, fasting, Christian fellowship, and the Lord's Supper.

By definition, piety is "a profound and controlling reverence for God" that determines everything we say, everything we do, and, indeed, everything we are.

WHERE TWO WAYS MEET

by Larry D. Smith

"We have reached a point where two ways meet." These words seem so relevant that one of our evangelists might speak them at IHC. If that should happen, his voice would be added to those of other troubled brothers and sisters who warn that the Conservative Holiness Movement is facing a major crisis in its identity. For, yes, as they believe, we do stand "at a point where two ways meet." Which way we choose will determine everything. For the first leads on to faithfulness and blessing; the other, to compromise and surrender.

But the caution that begins this article did not come from a CHM evangelist. It was issued in 1866 by Randolph S. Foster—devout Methodist pastor, teacher, and later bishop—to his own beloved church, which was then celebrating 100 years of phenomenal success. But in propelling Methodism up the social ladder to wealth and respectability, that success had cheapened its life and muffled its witness. "Our great dangers, as we see them," he wrote, "are assimilation to the world, neglect of the poor, substitution of the form for the fact of godliness, abandonment of discipline, a hireling ministry, an impure gospel, which, summed up, is a fashionable church."

But Methodism became exactly what Foster feared—a "fashionable church" conformed not to Christ but to the world! That, of course, is the usual trajectory of Christian Movements, caught up almost inevitably in what historians label "historical drift," as they move gradually away from their originating convictions. Think not only of Methodism, but also of Harvard University, the YMCA or any mainline denomination.

Nor are we exempt from such a fate, as the "Call to the Conservative Holiness Movement" acknowledges. In their introductory statements, its authors write: *"We share the distress of those who warn of 'historical drift,' spiritual apathy, and surrender to the depraved secular culture that surrounds us."* Now in Article V they speak again of "historical drift," pointing perceptively to the only remedy that will stop it. Consider carefully this compelling summons to "Methodist Piety" which we will now examine.

I. PRINCIPLE DECLARED: *Piety Essential*

By definition, piety is "a profound and controlling reverence for God" that determines everything we say, everything we do, and indeed, everything we are. For it deals with our personal relationship with God, built as it must be upon "the fear of the Lord," which as Scripture tells us, "is the beginning of wisdom" (Psalm 111:10). For sinners, the "fear of the Lord" eventuates in terror before His broken law and impending wrath; while for Christians, it is reverential awe for His holy character and mighty acts.

Love for God must become the motivating drive for every follower of Jesus, but it is certain that we shall never love Him until first we have come to fear Him. Remember also that as we welcome His overtures with open hearts and steadfast will, the Holy Spirit will use the fear of God to lead us to the love of God.

But even after this, the "fear of the Lord" as reverential awe will remain to brace, toughen and mold our love for Him, as they merge together in that rich Christian piety which provides the fertile soil in which all holiness must flourish. In contrast to sterile externalism, piety is rooted in inward principle and holy character, though it manifests itself in loving obedience and faithful service. At its very core it centers in a passionate desire and relentless pursuit for God Himself. *"As the hart panteth after the water brooks, so panteth my soul after thee, O God" (Psalm 42:1).*

No gift of our heritage is more precious than this focus on a rich personal relationship with God, and this is why Article V is a "Call to Methodist Piety." From the beginning, Wesleyans have underscored the necessity of really knowing God in authentic Christian experience, attested by a life that consistently demonstrates that reality. Generations of godly, earnest Christians—our spiritual forebears—have set the pattern before us: loving as Jesus loved in perpetual covenant with Him, as the "Call" reminds us, demonstrating "allegiance to the inner principle of 'jealous, godly fear,' commitment to disciplined discipleship, obedience to His holy law, dynamic growth in grace, and faithful use of the means of grace."

II. FAILURE ACKNOWLEDGED: *Piety Distorted*

Once Methodism was known as "Christianity in earnest." Granted, this is the mark of real Christians everywhere. But the piety demonstrated by so many of our spiritual ancestors—deep, sturdy, principled—was acknowledged even by those who did not share it. At our best, this "goodly heritage" is still richly displayed in the sanctity of hundreds of faithful saints who live the Jesus life among us.

At our worst, however, we have reduced piety to mere "external regulation and dutiful performance," as Article V reminds us. Granted, true religion is always ethical, for holy lives are inevitably the fruit of holy hearts. But it's easy to emphasize the results and neglect the principle that must produce them. *"For the kingdom of heaven is not meat and drink"—or any outward thing—"but righteousness, and peace and joy in the Holy Ghost" (Rom. 14:17).* Sometimes we've also embroidered our preaching by lists of forbidden items that at best are only the questionable opinions of those who lustily announce them.

It is in this context that Article V acknowledges the "'historical drift' among us," insisting that it will not be stopped "merely by enforcing traditional legislation but by vigorous and renewed insistence upon authentic relationship with God and passionate pursuit of Him." Without doubt, the "drift is on" across the CHM, as we are warned; and it is especially evident by the erosion of our historic "standards" of holy living. Once we stressed these to the neglect of the "inner principle" that must be their source. But now the pendulum swings the other way, and in many cases we are emphasizing neither the outward standards nor the "inner principle." Listen to the authors of the "Call," as they declare allegiance to both of these. "Gladly we reaffirm our traditional emphasis upon simplicity, modesty, stewardship, separation from the world and conscientious lifestyle; but all this must be within the warm and gracious context of loving what God loves and hating what God hates."

III. CORRECTION OFFERED: *Piety Renewed*

Fortunately, we have a superlative model for renewal in the old Methodist "school of piety" which for generations produced "Cadillac Christians," as Nazarene scholar Dr. Wes Tracy has observed. This was given formal structure in the General Rules of 1743 to which the "Call" makes specific reference. Holy purpose was foundational to the system, for all who sincerely wanted to follow Jesus were to evidence an earnest "desire to flee from the wrath to come and to be saved from their sins." They were placed in a structure of disciplined method that emphasized constant affirmation, mentoring and accountability. In this atmosphere, the Spirit produced men and women of extraordinary holiness—saints who had become so not by chance but by design. We may not be able to reproduce all the dimensions of this system, but we can call our people to renewed allegiance to the three commitments upon which it rested:

- ***Do "no harm, by avoiding evil of every kind."*** In other words, we must meet the "sin question" head on in our lives with honesty and determination. One of our problems is that our pulpits have grown timid in denouncing popular sin. But the heart must be thoroughly probed, and sin must be emphatically renounced. The world and its trinkets must be renounced "for the only way to Heaven is the royal way of the cross."

- ***Do "good, by being in every kind merciful after their power."*** So a Christian's life must be filled with flourishing good works, as he or she continually extends kindness to others, witnesses the love of Christ, and lives a faithful, disciplined life "by all diligence and frugality that the gospel be not blamed."

- ***Attend "upon all the ordinances of God."*** These are the means of grace, those outward words and deeds which God Himself has appointed as the conduits of His favor and which we must use systematically, lovingly and in faith. These are essential to Christian piety. There are five especially which are "instituted" for our nourishment in grace: (1) *prayer of every type*: personal, family and corporate; (2) *the Word of God*, Holy Scripture, which must be cherished, "read and expounded;"

(3) *Christian fellowship*, which unites us in holy bonds to other believers; (4) *Fasting* as a systematic and holy offering of self-denial; and (5) *Holy Communion*, which as Dr. Steve Harper reminds us, is "food for the journey home."

"We have reached a point where two ways meet." One leads to faithfulness and blessing, the other to compromise and surrender. Which of these will we take? Remember what Bishop Foster said about a "fashionable church"—a church conformed not to Christ but to the world. His warning is for us as surely as it was for our ecclesiastical great-grandmother who tragically chose to ignore it. Already there are signs of "'historical drift' among us," as the "Call" acknowledges. However, as it adds, its remedy is not found in legal codes and external duties, but in a dynamic renewal of what once made the Wesleyan Movement great—earnest and authentic Christian piety, which by definition is "a profound and controlling reverence for God" that determines everything we say, everything we do, and, indeed, everything we are.

A RETURN TO DISCIPLINED SPIRITUALITY

by Michael R. Avery

Article V of the "Call to the Conservative Holiness Movement" is a call to return to the principled piety that was fundamental to historic Methodism's success in spiritual formation. John Wesley's approach to the cultivation of holy character was nothing more than the methodical application of the ordinary means of grace that the Bible says are central to spiritual health and growth. Wesley defined the means of grace as the instruments appointed by God to *"convey to men preventing, justifying and sanctifying grace."* Wesley's list of these means included Scripture, prayer, the Lord's Supper, fellowship and fasting.

For some in the CHM, a call to reach into the treasures of our past is a call in the wrong direction. The assumption is that "everything has changed"; therefore, new approaches to the development of spiritual life are needed. I would dispute both parts of that equation. I readily acknowledge the constant change in the culture around us, but I firmly assert that basic human nature has not changed. Thus the fundamental human problem has not changed. Neither has the Biblical solution to that problem changed, nor has the effectiveness of that solution changed. Faith still comes by hearing and hearing by the Word of God. The ordinary means of grace are just as effective in today's 21st century church (if given a chance) as they were in those first Mediterranean house churches established by Paul centuries ago.

The CHM should not let go of its historic approach to the development of spiritual character. What it does need to do is to work on applying it with a better balance between discipline and dependence. It is easy to slip into the extreme of either approach. The extreme side of discipline is to over-emphasize the role of what we do to cultivate spiritual life. This position is characterized by the mentality of striving. It emphasizes knowledge, rules, rededication efforts and human activity while virtually ignoring God's grace extended through the enabling power of His Spirit. Its emphasis on "what do I need to do" can lead to the bondage of legalism.

On the other hand, the extreme side of dependence is to overemphasize God's role in our spiritual development to the neglect of any human initiative. This position is characterized by a "Jesus did it all" passivity. It stresses experience, the supernatural, and the person of the Holy Spirit to the neglect of human endeavor. The one side rolls up its sleeves and says, "God helps those who help themselves." The other side responds with, "It's all by grace." The CHM has generally fallen into the ditch of the former but is now showing signs of falling into the ditch of the latter.

The Biblical answer to this imbalance is that spiritual formation is both human and divine. Kenneth Boa stated it succinctly when he said that "discipline should work in concert with dependence, since grace is not opposed to effort but to earning." Paul places these elements back-to-back in Philippians 2:12-13: "So then, my beloved, ... work out your own salvation with fear and trembling; for it is God who is at work in you, both to will and to work for His good pleasure." Paul makes it clear that working out our salvation is not the same as working for it. He is also careful to balance this with the fact that God is active within us, accomplishing what all our learning and labor cannot.

The CHM must also guard diligently against the danger of just practicing the means of grace as ends in themselves. The "doing" of certain spiritual practices can create a subtle carnal smugness. The means of grace are never an end but merely the instruments through which God administers His grace. The means of grace were not given to satisfy our sense of "doing" but to transform us from the inside out! One can read the Bible faithfully yet fail to demonstrate the character it commends. One can be meticulous about his prayer time, yet fail to ever really pray or experience the oneness of true intercession. One can kneel at the altar to receive the communion elements as ritual only and completely miss the reality of His presence. Wesley warned about following the outward signs only without our hearts being renewed and enabled by the Holy Spirit.

Alan Redpath wisely noted that the conversion of a soul is the miracle of a moment, but the maturing into a great saint is the task of a lifetime. Our Methodist fathers understood this and modeled for us the art of disciplined spirituality like no one else in the last 100 years. It's our heritage—it should be our practice—it may be key to our renewal!

Chapter 6

A CALL TO AUTHORITY IN THE CHURCH

We call for renewed exposition of the Scriptural qualifications for leadership within the Church, corporate exhortation to beware the deceitfulness of sin, and Biblical obedience and submission to those whom God has made under-shepherds over us.

Those who have willingly joined a church or denomination and have given their pledge to obey the rules of membership ought to do so. They should honor and obey those in leadership and submit to the accountability and discipline of the church as outlined in the Scripture and the covenant of membership.

AUTHORITY IN THE CHURCH

by Michael R. Avery

The issue of authority in the church has come down to us through the centuries on a sea of blood and fire. The pages of church history tell the story. You can read of men slain by the sword or burned at the stake for questioning or acting contrary to the authority of the Church. At the heart of the Protestant Reformation was the issue of Church authority. The reformers declared that Christ alone was the head of the Church and the Bible was the ultimate authority. Many of our ancestors left their native lands to escape the heavy hand of a state church whose authority exploited rather than liberated the souls of men. Even today, there is still a vigorous discussion by churchmen, scholars, politicians and laymen as to the Church's authority on everything from birth control to baptism.

This discussion over authority in the church may sound somewhat benign and empty to most of the people who will read this chapter. Their religious world does not include popes, archbishops, bishops or councils! Churches within the holiness tradition function as self-governing communities or are affiliated with denominations that have a very limited form of top-down government. Neither approach, however, has allowed the holiness church to escape the discussion or the problem of authority. The "Call to the Conservative Holiness Movement," Article VI, states that the CHM has been marked by "the spirit of autonomy and even anarchy .... Too often ... we have exhibited rebellion against the authority structures which God Himself has established, boasting our independence of them, and refusing to submit to their godly discipline. This has been evidenced by continuing divisions among us, often over matters unconnected with allegiance to Scriptural truth."

This is a part of the "Call" with which I am not completely comfortable. The Movement obviously faces issues with authority, but I think the "Call" paints the CHM with too broad of a brush. I do not question the fact that there are those within the Movement who have exhibited a spirit of autonomy and rebellion. There are those whose self-serving ways and arrogant love for their own opinion have indeed spawned unnecessary division and bred much confusion.

I have watched with sadness as people have violated their word, ignored standards of ethical behavior, and broken membership vows while barely masking their obstinacy. We have all met an Absalom, an Adonijah or a Diotrephes who would not heed any counsel but their own or follow any path but one of their own making. But honestly, this has been the exception rather than the rule. On the contrary, most of the conservatives I know are more than willing to be led and are actually looking for leadership. They are quite willing to take very unpopular stands and live out countercultural lifestyles in obedience to their church and conscience. I see very little evidence that would indict them as rebels against Biblical authority or Biblically ordained authorities. This of course is my perception, but I believe it to be a fair one.

Rather than seeing them as rebels, I see something that may be construed as rebellion. I see confused, frustrated, and at times angry souls who are weary with leaders more willing to bow to church politics and fear than to lead with Biblical conviction and common sense. This weakness in leadership can and does produce reluctant and sometimes resistant followers, but none that should be called rebels. I see church attendees, both young and old, who lack a proper understanding of Biblical authority. I also see something else. I see a generational difference in how authority is viewed and understood. A failure to understand this generational difference may lead to labeling sincere, sanctified people as "rebels" who are only following their conscience and understanding as best as they can.

A BIBLICAL UNDERSTANDING OF AUTHORITY IN THE CHURCH

The concept of authority has fallen on bad times over the last few decades. In some places if you just say the word people react negatively. This should not surprise anyone since we have had a sad parade of politicians, policemen, professors, pastors and priests who have abused their authority and betrayed those who served under them. This abuse of authority has bred a culture of cynicism and suspicion. It has created an environment where good authority, God's authority, is regularly questioned. The cure is not to abandon the important role of authority in our culture but to carefully proclaim what God says in His Word about authority. My comments in this article are limited to authority in the Church.

The classic passage quoted in the "Call" and in most other discussions on church authority is Hebrews 13:17a: "Obey them that have the rule over you, and submit yourselves: for they watch for your souls, as they that must give account." This is a powerful principle that serious Christians seek to follow. It is also one that has been so terribly abused that it needs clarification.

First, no preacher, teacher or leader by virtue of his calling has been granted an inherent right to rule over other people. When I was ordained, I was given the authority "to preach the Word and administer the sacraments." The only authority that any pastor, teacher or church leader has is the delegated authority that comes through the Word of God and relates to the "spiritual guidance and soul safety" of those under his responsibility. (Read Wesley's sermon *On Obedience to Pastors.*)

Secondly, the application of Hebrews 13:17 applies only to those leaders who are faithful. All through Scripture we are warned to beware of false teachers and false shepherds. How do you judge the false from the true? You judge them by their fidelity to the Word of God, both in what they say and how they live. Those who teach the Word faithfully and live it faithfully deserve our respect and obedience. The pastor or leader who claims authority based on his position, or seeks to make his opinion equivalent to Scripture, or tries to use religion and false guilt to make one conform to his will is completely out of line with his Biblical authority.

Thirdly, the New Testament does not describe the kind of church organizations we have today. This does not mean it opposes today's denominational structures, but it just means that it primarily sees the visible church as a local community of believers led by a body of elders and deacons. However, it does speak quite forcefully to the issues of order, authority, submission, discipline and accountability. Those who have willingly joined a church or denomination and have given their pledge to obey the rules of membership ought to do so. They should honor and obey those in leadership and submit to the accountability and discipline of the church as outlined in the Scripture and the covenant of membership. If at some point, they decide not to do so, they should willingly and quietly withdraw from membership.

CHURCH AUTHORITY AND GENERATIONAL DIFFERENCES

The Greatest and Silent Generations

Christians born in the first half of the 20th century are referred to as the "Greatest" (1902-1924) and "Silent" (1925-1945) generations. They were born into what is called the "modern era." Their way of thinking, and subsequently their worldview, primarily reflects "modernity." They have an innate trust for the institutions of government, education and religion. They highly value rules for morality, decency and conformity. Issues of right and wrong fall easily and distinctly into black and white categories.

They understand the way the traditional church works, see membership as important, and think nothing of just doing whatever the church or church manual says. They do not need exhaustive exegesis or detailed explanations for demands placed upon them. This is not to say that they do not think, but it is only to say that these generations accept the rules without the need for "proof" or "explanation" because they believe in and trust the church and its leadership! Even in areas they personally do not understand or with which they do not fully agree, they are willing to go along and do what the church or pastor says because they trust the authority structures and believe it is important to obey and conform to what they are told.

As this way of thinking worked its way out in the more conservative churches, there developed a subtle emphasis on conforming to "group cultural rules of conduct." Conformity became more of a priority than the development of vital piety based on scriptural reflection. Living the rules with no grasp of the principle behind them became far too common. This resulted in at least two things worthy of observation: (1) externals became the focus or "proof" of real heart change; (2) it became far too easy to "look right" and thus "be right" without any internalization of character or sound Biblical understanding of why they did what they did. I hope this will not be misunderstood as an indictment of insincerity or an accusation of hypocrisy—it is not! It is an attempt to explain how this generation tended to think and act. I do not question their earnest desire to please God!

This is the generation that pulled out of the mainline holiness denominations and formed what is now called the Conservative Holiness Movement. This is the generation that embraced without question and lived without fear what their leaders and churches had taught them. When the "mother church" started changing values that had been held for decades, this generation voted with their feet and left the church. I believe their actions were rooted in two things: their convictions and their culture. Neither root is necessarily connected to rebellion. Were there rebels who opposed the authority of the church and who were involved in the "come out"? Of course! But the vast majority of come-outers were men and women of godly character who were simply standing by the things they had been taught.

The Boomer, Buster, and Millennial Generations

By the late 1960s and early '70s America had fully made a dramatic shift from the "modern era" to the "postmodern era." The second generation of conservative holiness people (Boomers) was influenced by both modern and postmodern thought. You can see the influence of both in the way they think and act. The third and fourth generations of conservatives were primarily influenced by post-modernism. Postmodern Christians think quite differently from those in the modern generation. The post-modern generation does not have a natural trust of the institutions of government, education and church.

On the contrary, they have a deep suspicion of these institutions and the power they wield. They reject “blind acceptance” of anything to the point of being cynical. They grew up in the “advertising age” and learned quickly you could not believe what you read on the cereal box or heard from the media. They look at all unsupported assertions with suspicion—especially those given in church. They do not simply swallow what is taught or preached. They ask questions and want answers. Just because the preacher says it is wrong doesn’t make it wrong for them. They want a clear, intellectually defensible, Biblical answer. If answers are not forthcoming, they reject the assertions. A large number of the early post-moderns were lost to the church because some leaders tragically confused “questions about Biblical truth” with “questioning the truth of the Bible” and classified them as compromisers or rebels.

The postmodern Christian rejects the carefully “air-brushed, compartmentalized, and rote cookie cutter religious expressions of the previous generations.” They prefer religious spontaneity and authenticity over mere appearances. This has caused a postmodern generation to be slow in accepting all the traditional lifestyle values and standards of the Conservative Holiness Movement. It’s not that they reject Biblical values, but rather they reject “cookie cutter” conformity for the sake of just “looking the part” or fitting into the culture.

They want to know the reason and see the value of the thing they are being asked to do. I don’t believe they have rejected the traditional values because those values lack veracity but because they have been given without explanation and applied without flexible common sense. Parents whose postmodern kids grew up in complete conformity to these values while at home are shocked when those same kids jettison those standards after leaving home. In some cases the rejection flows from a rebellious, worldly heart, but in many cases it does not. It flows from a heart that is seeking spiritual authenticity and from a mind that wants intellectual "buy in."

ADDRESSING THE PROBLEM

Rebellion is a strong word and should be used wisely. True rebellion against proper authority reveals a deeper rejection of God's authority and should be treated as such. That's why the Bible compares it to the sin of witchcraft and idolatry. Only the Holy Spirit can root out rebellion and replace it with submission by a radical change of one's heart. However, if we are dealing with generational ways of thinking, then we need to understand and respond accordingly. Christians of all generations desire authenticity. Authenticity begins with honesty. We must be honest with who we are, honest about our biases and prejudices, and honest in our interpretation and application of Scripture. Authenticity continues with a willingness to differentiate between what is Scripture and what is tradition, what is principle and what is preference, clarifying the role of both. However, authenticity also means that we refuse to conform to any cultural thought that is wrong and that we confront "unBiblical thinking" in every generation with the Word of God.

Romans 12:1-2 offers some remarkable insight: *"I beseech you therefore, brethren, by the mercies of God, that you present your bodies a living sacrifice, holy, acceptable to God, which is your reasonable service. And do not be conformed to this world, but be transformed by the renewing of your mind, that you may prove what is that good and acceptable and perfect will of God."* We can only replace bad thinking with Biblical thinking by the faithful application of the Word of God. The Holy Spirit can enlighten the mind with Biblical truth and change any way of thinking that does not align itself with God's point of view. The Holy Spirit can also discern between resistance to generational thinking and acting and rebellion to Biblically ordained authority. If real rebellion is present, then repentance and the relinquishment of self to God in holy surrender is the only cure for the rebel within. We must have both—the radical change of heart and the renewing of the mind—if we are to effectively deal with the problem of authority in this generation and in the ones to come.

STRUGGLING WITH SUBMISSION

by Larry D. Smith

Thirty-five years have passed since a conference of Christian leaders headed by Robert E. Webber, professor of theology at Wheaton College, issued "The Chicago Call." Evangelicals were in a period of growth, as they acknowledged, but were weakened by neglecting their roots in classical Christian orthodoxy. "There is therefore a pressing need to reflect upon the substance of the Biblical and historic faith," the writers said, "and to recover the fullness of this heritage." *Christianity Today* cautiously endorsed the document, while *Newsweek* devoted an entire "religion section" to its coverage.

Our own "Call to the Conservative Holiness Movement" is in this tradition, and some of our concerns are obviously the same. Others, however, are different, containing general principles applied to our own constituency. For ours is a specific summons "for the full and vigorous recovery of our heritage as Christians of Wesleyan conviction," urging "our entire Movement to unite with us joyfully in this commitment."

Article VI is a call to authority in the Church. As such, it echoes "The Chicago Call," which deplores "disobedience to the Lordship of Christ as expressed through authority in his church," and reminds its readers that this "has promoted a spirit of autonomy in persons and groups, resulting in isolationism and competitiveness, even anarchy, within the body of Christ." Our own struggles with authority have sometimes produced similar unfortunate responses. With these in mind, we turn now to Article VI with its plea for valid scriptural leadership in the Church.

I. PRINCIPLE DECLARED: *Authority Explained*

"Christ Our Lord has delegated powers of government to duly appointed officers in the Church, and we are commanded to obey them faithfully." These words that begin Article VI can hardly be disputed, though often they are ignored. Remember that the Church is the home of all Christ's faithful ones, where we live out our lives in union with Him and with one another, continuing "steadfastly in the apostles' doctrine and fellowship, and in breaking of bread, and in prayers" (Acts 2:42).

This is a spiritual and heavenly organism, to be sure; but it is also a physical and earthly one. While Jesus was here among us, He gathered around Himself His "little flock" as the nucleus of its fellowship; established the principles of its worship, ministry and structure; and commissioned His apostles to act in His name as its first pastors and superintendents. After He had ascended to His Father, they went everywhere, impassioned to "make disciples of the nations" and to bring those disciples into the community of the church where they submitted themselves to its guidance, discipline and instruction.

This was all by divine authority, of course, delegated by Christ to His apostles and by them "to faithful men who will be able to teach others also" (II Tim. 2:2). As we know, leadership is vastly important, and so Peter and Paul made certain that devout, wise and courageous leaders were in place in those infant congregations that they established.

Details may be elusive, but in general the New Testament pattern is apparent. As historian Dr. Earl Cairns informs us, there were two categories of leaders in the early church. First were "charismatic officials," which he identifies as "apostles, prophets, evangelists, pastors, and/or teachers"—all believers gifted by the Spirit to proclaim the gospel and guard its truth.

Second were "administrative officials"—elders or presbyters and deacons—whose "task was to carry out the governmental functions within a given church. The apostles laid down their qualifications and put them in office after their selection by the congregation." Qualifications for an elder are given in I Timothy 3:1-7 and in Titus 1:5-9 and for a deacon in Acts 6:3 and I Timothy 3:8-13. The elders were called to rule in the congregation and from their ranks came its pastors, while deacons were to assist the elders in "the dispensing of charity."

Submission to church authority was expected of every Christian, and by the Savior's own command, any believer who stubbornly and persistently "refused to hear the church" in the exercise of its disciplinary powers was to be considered "like a heathen and a tax collector" (Matthew 18:17)—that is, he was no longer a member of the Christian fellowship. *"Obey them that have the rule over you, and submit yourselves,"* commands the book of Hebrews, *"for they watch for your souls, as they that must give account, that they may do it with joy, and not with grief: for that is unprofitable for you" (Hebrews 13:17).*

II. FAILURE ACKNOWLEDGED: *Authority Disregarded*

Church authority—its extent and exercise—has often become an issue of flaming controversy. On one hand, it often has been tragically, even barbarously, misused. Recall the horrors of Medieval Catholicism with its arrogant claims to both the bodies and souls of men. For those who resisted, there was the rack, the noose, and the flame. Nothing better illustrates Lord Acton's words: *"Power corrupts; absolute power corrupts absolutely."*

In the 16th century Reformation, this arbitrary force was challenged and overthrown. Protestants reasserted the universal priesthood of all believers, though their leaders were careful to explain the Biblical guidelines for proper authority. Some of their descendants, however, established spiritual despotisms of their own; while in reaction, others declared their independence from any dominion except their own. So the children of the Reformation became known for their constant squabbles and their proliferating sects, each claiming its own ecclesiastical turf.

We in the CHM have had our share of "continued divisions among us, often over matters unconnected with allegiance to Scriptural truth," as Article VI reminds us. Sixty years ago our persistent protests against encroaching worldliness and increasing autocracy were registered in faithfulness to our understanding of the gospel. As such, they were legitimate and history has validated them. Our "mother churches" have drifted so far that we can hardly recognize them as the spiritual cradles of our youth.

But it is also true that once we had thrown off the old loyalties, we found it difficult to establish new ones. This is made worse by the long-established "radical individualism" of American culture, as well as by the postmodern distrust of institutions either secular or religious. Perhaps these have all contributed to "the spirit of autonomy and even anarchy" that is deplored in Article VI.

"Our spiritual philosophy has become warped," declared A.W. Tozer of American evangelicalism; "our sense of belonging has gone from us; we recognize no authority, obey no rules, take no vows, are almost altogether undisciplined and feel no sense of loyalty." He was not speaking specifically to the CHM, of course; but still his indictment provides a solemn warning for us all.

III. CORRECTION OFFERED: *Authority Reaffirmed*

"Yea, all of you be subject one to another, and be clothed with humility: for God resisteth the proud and giveth grace to the humble" (I Pet. 5:5). Here is the mutual submission that we owe to one another in the Church. But this is not all that is required. *"Obey them that have the rule over you, and submit yourselves: for they watch for your souls" (Hebrews 13:17).* Here is the personal submission that we owe to the Church's leaders.

To explain and affirm that authority we now summarize these principles foundational to it:

- ***Delegation.*** To the Church which He has established, our Lord has delegated His own authority which is exercised by duly-appointed officials who act in His name and on His behalf.
- ***Qualification.*** In Scripture He has established the qualifications for these officials: godliness, sobriety, earnestness, diligence, family discipline and spotless reputation. Acting reverently in His presence and relying upon His guidance, the congregation selects its leaders from those who thus are clearly qualified.
- ***Limitation.*** These officials are to exercise their authority in a spirit of fidelity, love, and humility, always limited to the proper sphere of spiritual concern that the church has committed to them.

- ***Service.*** Church officials are to serve God and His people humbly, faithfully and lovingly, "taking the oversight thereof, not by constraint, but willingly; not for filthy lucre, but of a ready mind; neither as being lords over God's heritage, but being ensamples to the flock" (I Pet. 5:2-3).
- ***Obedience.*** By divine command we are to submit to the spiritual authority which these leaders exercise in God's name, offering them our affirmation, our prayers, and our support.
- ***Accountability.*** We are accountable to these leaders. But they also are accountable to us, and the Church must provide structures to which they give answer and by which they may be deposed for just cause. Remember, too, that all of us are accountable to God before whom we soon shall stand in judgment.

Granted, the "Call to the Conservative Holiness Movement" will never appear in *Christianity Today* or *Newsweek*. It did appear in *God's Revivalist*, however, urging us to "support that authority in the church" that God Himself has established. "Be assured of one thing," John Wesley tells us. "The more conscientiously you obey your spiritual guides, the more powerfully God will apply the word which they speak in His name to your health. The more powerfully will He water what is spoken with the dew of His blessing; and the more proofs will you have, not only what they speak, but the Spirit of your Father who speaketh in them."

Chapter 7

A CALL TO CORPORATE WORSHIP

We call for the renewal of our corporate worship, based in the mandates of Scripture and in the tradition of evangelical orthodoxy, centered in the faithful ministry of Word and Sacrament.

One dimension of our worship, then, points to heaven, as we speak faithfully and reverently to God, while the other points to earth, as God speaks faithfully and transformationally to us.

ANGELS TEACH US TO WORSHIP GOD

by Larry D. Smith

"Glory to God in the highest!" We hear again the Christmas angels as they chant Jehovah's praise. *"On earth peace, good will toward men!"* For our salvation He had given us His Son, the Word made flesh; and now He sends a choir from Heaven to celebrate that Gift of gifts with worship. Ponder humbly the dimensions of that worship because they provide God's pattern for our own. "Glory ascends to Heaven, and peace descends to earth," as Daniel Whedon comments. "Such is the reconciliation between God and man."

Thus angels teach us how to worship. *"Glory to God in the highest!"* Here is what we offer Him. *"On earth peace, good will toward men!"* Here is what He offers us. One dimension of our worship, then, points to Heaven, as we speak faithfully and reverently to God, while the other points to earth, as God speaks faithfully and transformationally to us. These dimensions—one ascending, the other descending—are essential to all Christian worship, whether the private devotions offered daily by the individual believer or the public devotions offered weekly by the entire congregation. Thus in classic definition, *Christian worship is the glorification of God and the sanctification of humanity.*

CORPORATE WORSHIP DEFINED

"Corporate worship is the exalted glory and central pulse of every Christian congregation. At its core, worship is the adoration

of God, Holy, Blessed, and Undivided Trinity; and by apostolic mandate, it is to be conducted with decency and order."

In these words, worship is defined and affirmed as the essential function of every congregation—the very pulse and rhythm of its life. For not only is the entire church a holy temple (II Cor. 6:16; Eph. 2:1922), "offering up on every shore, / Her pure sacrifice of love," as an old hymn reminds us, but so is every one of its local gatherings. For wherever Christians meet—in Gothic cathedral or clapboard storefront—they stand on holy ground, one of Heaven's "outer courts" where God is adored, praised, and exalted; even as He is by "angels and archangels and all the company of Heaven." Someday we shall join them there, but until then we join them here. So it's true—all our worship in this life is rehearsal for worship in the life to come. If this is so, as someone has suggested, we had better get it right!

"Yes, worship of the living God is man's whole reason for existence," as A.W. Tozer insists. "That is why we are born, and that is why we are born again from above. That is why we were created, and that is why we have been recreated. That is why there was a genesis at the beginning, and that is why there is a regenesis called regeneration." What is true of Christians personally is true of Christians corporately. For as Tozer continues, "Worship is also why there is a church. The Christian church exists to worship God first of all. Everything else must come second or third or fourth or fifth."

With profound reverence, therefore, we bow each Lord's Day in the Lord's house with the Lord's people to adore Him, the Supreme Majesty of Heaven, "high and lifted up" in the awesome Unity of His Being and in the sublime Trinity of His Persons. "Holy, Holy, Holy, Lord God of Hosts!" In doing this, we unite our hearts and voices in the Church's continual "sacrifice of praise and thanksgiving," which in Heaven He accepts through the mediation of Jesus our great High Priest and which on earth He hallows by the mediation of the Holy Spirit our Sanctifier, who transforms us with "ever-increasing splendor" into the likeness of His Son (II Cor. 3:18).

CORPORATE WORSHIP IMBALANCED

"As Wesleyans we have a twofold heritage in Christian worship. On the one hand is the warmth and earnestness of fervent and joyful devotion. On the other is the sober restraint of form, dignity and tradition. Both are essential. Too often, however, we have emphasized the first and neglected the second." So as the "Call" makes clear, our problem is a lack of balance, as are most of our problems.

What happens on Sunday morning throughout the CHM differs from church to church, but almost always it is shaped by the freewheeling exuberance of the frontier camp meeting which nourished our beginnings. Granted, in most places this exuberance is now greatly diminished, but many still remember it with longing. In any case, our worship pattern centers in fervent preaching, personal testimonies and rousing altar calls—all within an atmosphere of warm-hearted emotional response. This is augmented with continuous appeals to personal spiritual experience played out in personal feelings, personal impressions and personal reactions.

This appeal to the emotional, individual and experiential is one aspect of our heritage—the subjective element so necessary to all human-divine encounter. At its best, it has been used mightily by the Spirit to make Jesus real to yearning saints caught up in those blessed moments when "Heaven comes down our souls to greet, / While glory crowns the mercy seat." Frankly I wish we had more such moments. When I experienced them as a child, they made me long to be a real Christian.

But whenever revivalistic worship is divorced from "the sober restraint of form, dignity, and tradition," the second gift of our heritage, it drifts easily into irreverent familiarity and mushy sentimentality, exalting feelings to the neglect of mind and will. Even worse, this subjective emphasis tends to downgrade the solid objective foundations in Christian doctrine so essential to our hope in Christ. So worship becomes me-centered rather than God-centered, as our thoughts are fixed almost exclusively upon our "personal relationship" with God rather than upon God Himself "high and lifted up" in transcendent glory.

Too often this has been our experience. We sing choruses and gospel songs that point more to us and our joys and burdens than about God and the worship that He calls us to offer Him. We talk endlessly about our own "personal walk" with Him but seldom read lessons from His Word as regular acts of worship, though the preacher usually reads a few verses as a prelude to his sermon, which often is more exhortation than exegesis. We schedule many "specials"—usually vocal but sometimes instrumental—that "bless" and "inspire" us; but we neglect baptism and the Lord's Supper, the two sacraments of the gospel which Jesus Himself commanded us faithfully to observe.

CORPORATE WORSHIP RENEWED

For good reason, then, we are summoned to renew our worship. Many across America's religious spectrum have tried to do this by adding popular entertainment, pumped-up music, and "seeker sensitive" gimmicks. But these are shallow substitutes for the rich spiritual reality that brings honor to Heaven and sanctity to earth. What we must do, rather, as the "Call" suggests, is to ground our worship firmly in "the mandates of Scripture and in the tradition of evangelical orthodoxy," centered in what Christian worship has always been—"the faithful ministry of Word and Sacrament." In other words, we must pattern our efforts by what the Bible teaches as it has been practiced by generations of faithful Christians. None of this will be successful, however, unless the Spirit breathes new life, purpose, and excitement as we do His bidding. Oh, that He would rend the heavens and come down!

We now make these four affirmations that will guide our efforts:

1. Worship is centered in God. Our conduct of public services—our music, our prayers, our sermons, and whatever else we do—is a sacrifice to God, the Holy Triune One, whom we adore and magnify. This means that we cultivate an atmosphere of profound reverence and joyful openness that excludes all that is merely clownish, sensational, and entertaining.

2. Worship is objective in content. This means it is shaped by solid truth revealed in Holy Scripture, confessed in ancient creeds, proclaimed in faithful preaching, and rehearsed in soaring hymns that point the Church to its doctrinal foundations. This is not to deny that certain choruses enhance our worship, but they must never replace the majestic hymns of our Wesleyan heritage. These hymns solidify our faith in God and lift us to Him. Thus, worship appeals primarily to our mind and to our will, but as the Spirit moves graciously among us, our emotions are often roused to warm subjective response.

3. Worship is corporate in nature. Through the Spirit's mediation, worship brings together the devotions of each member of the congregation into one collective offering lifted up in love to Heaven. Thus we sing *congregational* hymns, have *responsive* readings, and join in *unison* repetition of the Lord's prayer, the creeds, and other acts of prayer and praise. Sunday worship is no time for talent shows, dramatic presentations, musical concerts or me-centered personal focus.

4. Worship is complete in content. So Scripture, the great pattern that God has given, points to adoration, thanksgiving, confession and supplication as the basic elements of common worship, even as they are of individual worship. Moreover, the preaching of the Word and the celebration of the Lord's Supper—provide its recurring pattern, as they have since the earliest Christians "continued steadfastly in the apostles' doctrine and fellowship, and in breaking of bread, and in prayers" (Acts 2:42).

"Glory to God in the highest." We hear again the Christmas angels as they chant Jehovah's praise. *"On earth peace, good will toward men!"* So they teach us to worship God.

CHRISTIAN WORSHIP

by Michael R. Avery

I love the Church! I love the branch of the Church called the Holiness Movement where God has placed me! However, neither my love for the Church nor for that part which I serve has made me blind to the spots and wrinkles of either. The "Call to the Conservative Holiness Movement" is an attempt to restate the strengths of that tradition, to recognize weaknesses that have developed over time, and to dialogue on how to restore what is vital to its future.

Article VII is a call to the CHM to evaluate honestly its present practices of corporate worship. The importance of such an evaluation is underscored by the importance of the act of worship itself. The Westminster Confession reminds us that man's chief end is to "glorify God and enjoy Him forever." Scripture teaches us that worship is vital to our "creature hood" and central to our faith. If things are not healthy in our worship experience, then things are not healthy in our church no matter how well we do other things.

Warren Weirsbe has defined worship as the believers' response of all that they are—mind, emotions, will, and body—to what God is and says and does. In the best Methodist/holiness tradition, worship engages the whole person in a well-balanced blend of joyful celebration and reverential awe that is often reciprocated by the manifest presence of God. When worship succeeds in this fashion, I know of no other worship tradition that enables men to worship God any better.

CHM WORSHIP STRENGTHS

Conservative holiness people are singing people. Praise is central to worship. Music in the present-day Church is the primary form of praise. So music and worship are inextricably connected. Music marks the worship found in both the Old and New Testaments. It has marked the Church across the centuries and around the world. Step inside the average CHM church, and you will hear warm-hearted, enthusiastic, highly-engaged singing that is often reinforced with such expressions of praise as "Glory to God," "Hallelujah," and "Praise the Lord." Holiness people know how to worship in song!

Conservative holiness people deeply desire God's presence. All Christians claim the promise, "For where two or three are gathered together in my name, there am I in the midst of them" (Matt. 18:20). Holiness people, however, truly expect the presence of God to be evident. Their zeal and longing for His presence is often rewarded with a gracious visitation of His manifest presence.

Conservative holiness people have a keen sensitivity to the work of the Holy Spirit. In the best Wesleyan/holiness tradition, order and structure are always present. But there is also present a willingness to let the Spirit of God set aside the planned program if need be to accomplish His own sovereign purposes.

Conservative holiness people have a strong love for good preaching. The preaching event still takes a very high place in Holiness Movement worship. Holiness people read their Bibles and carry them to church. They want good preaching, respond to good preaching, and show sincere respect for the preacher who gives them the unadulterated Word of God.

CHM WORSHIP WEAKNESSES*

Too many services lack thoughtful planning. Growing up in the CHM, I was taught to be suspicious of liturgy, only to discover that every church follows a liturgy, whether it's a good one or a bad one, written or unwritten. This fear or neglect of careful planning produces a worship experience that lacks continuity (it is very disjointed and broken apart by things that could be avoided with minimal planning) and is random in its forward movement. It will fail to lead the congregant in a meaningful worship experience. Churches who have consistently good worship experiences are those where the worship service is thoughtfully planned, intentionally structured, steeped in prayer, and executed under the leadership of the Holy Spirit. Careful planning does not hinder the freedom of God's Spirit to work. Actually, it gives Him a reliable framework through which He can inspire worship and minister grace to His people.

Too many holiness churches have stressed feeling and experiencing God to the neglect of worshiping and glorifying God. Jesus taught us to worship in spirit and in truth. Worship must have both heart and head. Worship must engage emotions and thought. Truth without emotion produces dead orthodoxy. On the other hand, emotion without truth produces empty frenzy and cultivates shallow people who refuse the discipline of rigorous thought. Many sincere attempts to feel God near have lost this balance and have opened the door to fleshly emotionalism, calling it worship.

We have allowed worship to become something we do for our benefit rather than something we offer to God. This twist in focus has turned church into a performance event where we are the recipients. We want the songs to bless us, the prayers to comfort us, and the sermon to help us feel better about our condition. True worship is not self-centered, but God-centered. In true worship, God is the audience and we are the performers! Robert Coleman said it well, "Worship is the adoring response of the creature to the infinite majesty of God. While it presupposes submission to Him, to worship, in the highest sense, is not supplication for needs, or even thanksgiving for blessings, but the occupation of the soul with God Himself."

Prayer is generally fervent but often lacks substance. The offering of prayers has always been a vital part of Christian worship and certainly an important part of worship within the CHM tradition. Prayer is so intimate and personal that we have been hesitant to critique it. But as a central part of worship, public prayer should be evaluated. Public prayer or the pastoral prayer is different from our private time with God. It should evidence thought and preparation. I know a pastor who spends a considerable amount of time writing out his Sunday morning prayer. He takes the responsibility of leading his congregation to God seriously. His prayers contain a wonderful balance of adoration, petition and confession. They are steeped in Biblical language. They have forward Movement that is orderly and thoughtful. But more importantly, they are deep and powerful. On the other hand, unless one has trained himself in the art of public prayer, the average extemporaneous prayer tends to be shallow, directionless and often repetitious. Careful thought and preparation will not rob us of authentic sincere prayer. On the contrary, it will help us truly to attain it!

There is a noticeable lack of Scripture. We have left Scripture out of our present-day worship services. Rarely do you find a CHM church that gives attention to Scripture readings, calls to worship and responsive readings. Quite often, you do not even need your Bible for the sermon! Often Scripture reading is ignored in the name of "saving time." However, I believe we fail here for two reasons. First, we think what we have to say is more important and effective than the public reading of Scripture. Second, we are poor readers. One only has to hear a good reader lift up the Scripture to know the power of the read Word!

TOO IMPORTANT TO IGNORE

There may be something optional about how one worships, but worship itself is not optional. Corporate worship is the exalted purpose and central pulse of every Christian congregation. If you are not worshiping, you are not having church—you are just holding a shabby religious sideshow and calling it worship. What will it take to motivate you and your church to rebuild the altar of true worship? Think about it. There is too much at stake not to do so!

**I asked a group of pastors and church leaders within the CHM to give me a list of what they believed were the worship weaknesses of the CHM. Their lists were remarkably similar and were used to develop the list in this chapter.*

Chapter 8

A CALL TO CONSISTENT DISCIPLESHIP

We call for a commitment to equip our laity for the work of the ministry, for the establishment of solidly Wesleyan curricula for systematic discipleship, and for the implementation of these training methods in all our churches.

The conversion of a soul is the miracle of a moment, but the maturing of a great saint is the task of a lifetime.

DEVELOPING DEEP CHRISTIANS

by Michael R. Avery

If you had the opportunity to attend a public event at the United States Military Academy in West Point, New York, you would see an impressive group of young men and women who are being prepared to go anywhere in the world under any circumstances and to swing into action the minute their boots hit the ground. They are military officers in the making. Upon their graduation they will be commissioned as *"leaders of character committed to the values of Duty, Honor, and Country ... prepared for a career of professional excellence and service to the Nation as an officer in the United States Army."*

Is there any similarity between what happens at West Point and what happens at your local church? Does your local church have a systematic process for producing mature Christian disciples who can pray, share their faith, explain the Bible, defend their doctrine, put the well-being of others ahead of their own, stand up under persecution, or do whatever they need to do for Christ's Kingdom wherever their feet hit the ground?

You don't have to answer that question because we already *know* the answer. The church is struggling to produce men and women who fit the Biblical standard of *spiritual maturity.* We are failing to produce people of depth. People who are deep in spiritual character, deep in faith, deep in prayer, deep in love for God and others! This process is actually called discipleship, and it is not happening in the average church.

The "Call to the Conservative Holiness Movement" speaks to this in Article VIII. It decries the fact that we have *"largely abandoned our Methodist system of spiritual formation and forgotten how to fulfill our Lord's command to make disciples. We have sought revival without preparing to preserve its fruits. We have emphasized spectacular conversions and neglected the Biblical necessity of disciplined growth in faith, virtue, knowledge, self-control, perseverance, godliness, brotherly kindness and love."* The end result is that the CHM suffers from too many shallow Christians.

I felt the "push back" and irritation from a lot of conservatives as soon as that last sentence formed on the page in front of me! But, alas, it must stand! Conservatives face the normal fallout of failing to disciple their people. However, they also face another subtle danger of appearing to be deep rather than actually being deep! It is very easy for us to look spiritual while actually being as shallow as the carnal Corinthians.

Being deep is more than just knowing and honoring the Bible in visible ways (especially those that make us look spiritual in our setting). That can happen while failing to demonstrate the character it commands. One can be meticulous, even legalistic, about his tithe and yet fail ever to develop the spirit of generosity. One can dress modestly and still have a sensual spirit. Sheer knowledge of the Bible doesn't make one godly. The mere application of a few visible commands doesn't mean we have cultivated holy character. One can read the Bible daily, acquire significant amounts of Biblical knowledge, adopt standards of dress and behavior, yet have no straight-line correspondence between that and real Christlikeness. One can embrace the conservative creed, adopt its lifestyle principles, and learn the language of the "old-fashioned way" and still be shallow.

Many conservative leaders readily admit that the CHM is not getting the job done when it comes to the discipleship of new believers. Some recognize that we also are not taking the second step and engaging in the lifelong mentoring process that creates deep Christians. Few, if any, are talking about the problems that result from not discipling—a problem that Thomas Bergler calls the *"Juvenilization of Christianity."* When converts are not placed on a deliberate trajectory toward spiritual maturity, the character traits of duty, discipline, scriptural living, holy habit, holy affections, denying oneself, sacrificial loving and giving—all traits of mature Christians—they are decoupled from normal adulthood and moved down the road to some future time that may or may not arrive. The shallowness that is left is a self-centered, emotionally driven and intellectually empty faith that is focused more on "being fulfilled" than on "being faithful."

DISCIPLESHIP THE ONLY CURE!

New believers do not develop into deep Christians on their own any more than a little boy playing soldier becomes a great general on his own. We know this from church history and from personal experience. More importantly, we know this because the Bible gives us examples of how God Himself develops deep people. Jesus chose to spend the majority of His time discipling His twelve disciples. With only a three-year public ministry, I think it remarkable that He made a limited number of public appearances and preached relatively few sermons while investing the vast majority of His time in the men who followed Him. Watching this process unfold in the Gospels, it looks like just three years of walking, talking and eating with them. But in reality Jesus was building character, teaching them how to think as He thought, and reshaping the spiritual parts of their lives in such a way that would prepare them to live, suffer, and die for His Kingdom. This three-year investment had such exponential results that we still feel its effect today!

Christians who are spiritually deep people have gone through God's discipleship program. Whether it is Moses, Paul, John Wesley or John Doe, all deep people have three things in common. *Each has been cultivated by God through direct encounters, experienced the character development made possible by difficult circumstances, and has been exposed to deliberate mentoring by resourceful people.*

DIVINE ENCOUNTERS

The journey to becoming a deep person begins with a direct encounter with God. This is what the Church has called a person's conversion. No man can or even wants to become a deeply spiritual person who has not had a heart change wrought by the Holy Spirit. The Apostle Paul's experience on the road to Damascus was such an encounter. He was not only converted to Christ but given his life's calling. But there are other encounters with God. Some are very personal like Jacob's encounter with God at Peniel. That encounter gave Jacob a painful insight into his own carnal self and left him with a changed nature, a new name, and a life marked forever by an amazing touch from God.

Other encounters give us insight into the character and nature of God. Moses' encounter with God in Exodus 33 is an example of this. Moses had asked to see God's "face" (glory) and was told he would be permitted to see God's "goodness." What he asked for and what he received were quite different—a difference that is important. Dennis Kinlaw clarifies the difference with this comment, "You can have a spiritual experience that is very exciting and yet is contentless, or you gain an insight into the character of the Eternal that will change you forever." These encounters with God along the path of life are crucial to our development into deep people.

DIFFICULT CIRCUMSTANCES

As A.W. Tozer reminds us, "It is doubtful whether God can use a man greatly until first He wounds him deeply." In my almost forty years of walking with the Lord, I have been blessed to receive numerous words of appreciation and kindness. They have encouraged me and strengthened me in my work and walk. However, it has been the difficult circumstances of life, the harsh winds of trial and adversity, the unjust words of a foe, and the dark night of the soul that have done more to shape my character in Christlikeness than almost anything else. Deep people have been discipled by the character-shaping experience of difficult circumstances.

DELIBERATE MENTORING

Deep people are not self-formulating. Their lives are enriched by the counsel and wisdom of others. All of us need godly men and women who have experienced life and know God intimately to speak into our lives. Most often this comes in a person-to-person encounter. However, it may take the form of books or other spiritual resources. Moses had his father-in-law Jethro. Paul had his traveling partner Barnabas. Timothy had his spiritual father Paul. Wesley had his books, his brother and his Moravian friends. The early Methodists had the class meeting—a system that produced a steady stream of deep people. Tozer had the writings of the early Church Fathers and the Mystics. Deep people will always have someone in their life who affirms, instructs, corrects and holds them accountable.

THE IMPLICATIONS OF FAILING TO DISCIPLE

The CHM must stop using the altar as the primary place of spiritual formation. The altar can certainly be a place of spiritual transformation and decision. But spiritual formation and growth takes place in the discipleship phase of Christian living. The work of discipling believers and mentoring deep people can no longer be a point of mere discussion. It must begin in earnest. Our failure to disciple deep people has already created a scarcity of spiritual leaders who have that blend of maturity, wisdom and balance that is needed to lead effectively. If we do not reverse the trend, the CHM could well be headed into irrelevance.

Alan Redpath wisely noted that the conversion of a soul is the miracle of a moment, but the maturing of a great saint is the task of a lifetime. Our Methodist fathers understood this and modeled for us the art of making disciples like no one else in the last 200 years. It's our heritage—it should be our practice—and it may be the key to our survival!

SOLDIER OF THE CROSS

by Larry D. Smith

"Am I a soldier of the cross / A follower of the Lamb?" These words sung so often in the church of my childhood remain etched upon my heart, still probing my conscience, rousing my courage, and bracing my will. *"Am I a soldier of the cross?"* Sooner or later each of us must confront this question. It is probing, personal, and pointed, to be sure, though not more so than Jesus' own imperative: *"If anyone wishes to come after Me, let him deny himself and take up his cross daily, and follow me."*

To follow Jesus, then, is to center our lives in unconditional allegiance to Him and to His service. *"No one putting his hand to the plow and looking back is fit for the Kingdom of God,"* as He declared. If these words mean anything at all, they mean no fudging, no trifling, no selling out! For Jesus wasn't interested just in making converts like those fickle recruits described by Tom Paine during our Revolution as "sunshine patriots" and "summer soldiers." Granted, He sometimes takes us on when we are like that, but His relentless purpose is to fashion us into dedicated, devout and determined disciples—yes, "soldiers of the cross." "Sure, I must fight if I would reign / Increase my courage, Lord! / I'll bear the toil, endure the pain / Supported by Thy word!"

But not only does Jesus call us to be His disciples, but He also calls us to fill the world with them. *"Go therefore and make disciples of all the nations, baptizing them in the name of the Father and the Son and the Holy Spirit, teaching them to observe all things that I have commanded; and lo, I am with you always, even to the end of the age."*

Here, of course, is the Great Commission of Matthew 28—the unaltered standing orders given to the Church for all the ages. So it is vastly significant that Article VIII of the "Call to the Conservative Holiness Movement" appeals directly to its specific mandates. We consider this now, "A Call to Consistent Discipleship," for it confronts our tragic failure to develop consistent systems used by the Spirit to mentor and mature faithful "soldiers of the cross."

DISCIPLESHIP ESSENTIAL

Christ's ancient Church was a fiery evangelistic Movement, proclaiming "repentance and remission of sins" (Luke 24:47), as Jesus had commanded. Yet His earliest believers also "realized that the central thrust of the Great Commission was discipleship accomplished through baptism and teaching, so they largely invested their time and energy in systematically teaching new converts the whole counsel of God and equipping them for ministry." Remember how St. Paul counseled Timothy (2 Tim. 2:2), "And the same things which you have heard from me in the presence of many witnesses, these entrust to faithful men who will be able to teach others also."

Thus Theophilus was "entrusted" with St. Luke's careful account of Jesus' ministry so that he might know "the exact truth about the things you have been taught" (Luke 1:3-4), and Apollos, after being "instructed in the way of the Lord," gave himself to "speaking and teaching accurately the things concerning Jesus" (Acts 18:25). This process of instruction soon became normative throughout the Church, established in the Catechumenate, "dating substantially from apostolic times," as the brilliant historian

Philip Schaff informs us. This was to prepare new converts to receive baptism, and thus formal membership in the Church, by "special instruction under teachers called 'catechists.'" Surviving from the First or Second Centuries is the Didache, an invaluable manual of catechetical instruction based on the Sermon on the Mount. Its purpose was to educate, mentor and strengthen new Christians, "equipping them for ministry," to use the words of the "Call."

We Wesleyans once had a system that magnificently accomplished the same purposes. "Once upon a time the Lord raised up a man named John Wesley," as Nazarene scholar, Dr. Wes Tracy, reminds us. "He and his spiritual comrades started a religious Movement to produce holy Christians, believers who were sanctified through and through, wholly given to God and to service." Holy ends must be produced by holy means, however; and so they erected a methodical system designed for this purpose; and this is why they were called Methodists. "They met in societies, classes, bands, and mentoring and twinsoul pairs to help each other toward holiness of heart and life. They met in societies two or three times a week for worship and instruction. They met once a week in classes of twelve to teach, encourage, and pray for each other."

> "It was a true covenant community of faith," Tracy explains. "They even called their Movement a 'connexion,' for the members were connected with each other in the quest for holiness. ... The people practiced family worship twice a day. They organized backsliders' bands for the spiritually weak. They observed the love feast. If hard feelings, misunderstandings, or some other offense had come between them and a brother or sister, they would break the love feast bread together and mend the relationships. In addition, the people conducted prayer meetings. They

> preached on street corners, in fields, in churches and chapels. They took Communion every chance they got. They ministered to the poor and needy. ... If you were not willing to 'spend and be spent' for the poor, you were regarded as having not 'one grain' of true faith."

In this loving but structured atmosphere of prayer, activity and discipline, they submitted to spiritual examination, grew in "habituated virtue," entered into the experience of perfect love, ministered to the lost, shook their world for Jesus, and at last entered Heaven. "The people that this Movement molded often became spiritual giants, models of holiness, heroes of sacrificial service—Cadillac Christians you might say."

DISCIPLESHIP NEGLECTED

Thank God for the Cadillac Christians who still walk among us. But in great measure the CHM has no systematic process for advancing believers in maturity and holiness, except perhaps a continual round of altar going enforced by repeated pulpit exhortation. By the law of diminishing returns, this often plays out in disappointment and frustration, and the results have often been tragic and even fatal. Holy ends still must be produced by holy means, and long ago we deconstructed the holy means that once made Methodism known as "Christianity in earnest," as Dr. Chalmers described it.

Consider then the specific acknowledgments that the "Call" makes so forcefully. There are exceptions, of course, but in general (1) "we have largely abandoned our Methodist system of spiritual formation and have forgotten how to fulfill our Lord's command to make disciples"; (2) "we have sought revival without preparing to preserve its fruits"; (3) "we have emphasized spectacular conversions and neglected the Biblical necessity of disciplined growth in faith, virtue, knowledge, self-control, perseverance, godliness, brotherly kindness and love"; and (4) we have made little attempt to establish "any systematic plan for incorporating new converts into the visible body of Christ through baptism and instruction."

DISCIPLESHIP RENEWED

Genuine revival is desperately needed to heal our fractured relationships, sweep away our spiritual apathy, and confront our increasing worldliness. Yet revival is not enough. For if we are to see solid, saintly, and seasoned "soldiers of the cross" flourishing among us, we must reconnect with the foundational principles of our movement. Otherwise, we will dwindle into "a rope of sand," as George Whitefield confessed of his own uninstructed converts.

"We call therefore ... for a commitment to equip our laity for the work of the ministry, for the establishment of a solidly Wesleyan curricula for systematic discipleship, and for the implementation of these training methods in all our churches." Let me add these specific points of focus:

Authentic Relationship. Our pulpits must resound with a clear-cut insistence on really knowing God through a transformative encounter with Him, nourished by the disciplines of joyful and consistent piety, and deepened by the sanctifying work of the Holy Spirit. Christian relationship must begin in radical conversion.

Holy Covenant. We must reestablish a sense of community bound together by holy vows to God and to one another in perpetual covenant, publicly formalized in holy baptism. Nothing is more basic than these commitments spelled out in John Wesley's General Rules: (1) renounce all known sin; (2) do "good ... of every possible sort, and as far as possible, to all men"; and (3) use "all the ordinances of God"—that is, the instituted means of grace, which are prayer, the Scriptures, Christian fellowship, fasting and the Holy Communion.

Faithful Catechesis. Every congregation should inaugurate methods of instructing our people in holy Scripture and Christian doctrine, certainly in converts' classes, but also in such venues as Sunday school, midweek services and weekend seminars. Traditional catechisms cover every essential area of Christian truth, but especially for children, they focus on the Ten Commandments, the Apostles' Creed and the Lord's Prayer. We must issue our catechisms again and instruct our people in their contents.

Structured Accountability. We must recover our own historic emphasis on system, rhythm and discipline in the formation of holy character. We should consider again the use of small groups for affirmation and accountability like the old Methodist class meetings, gathering voluntarily on a weekly basis. Each of us should be part of a loving and structured system in which we "watch over one another in love," and at least occasionally answer the question asked so often in those old class meetings, "Brother, Sister, how does your soul prosper?"

"Am I a soldier of the cross?" This question needs to ring out clearly again through the CHM—and bringing back Watts fine old hymn would be a good place to begin. For to follow Jesus is to center our lives in unconditional allegiance to Him and to His service. It is the duty of His whole Church—and specifically the duty of the CHM—to establish holy means and systematic methods to help every believer develop into a dedicated, devout and determined disciple of Jesus—yes, a "soldier of the cross."

Chapter 9

A CALL TO CHRISTIAN SOCIAL WITNESS

We call for renewed commitment to Christian social witness. This means that we will lovingly and forcefully proclaim Christ's power to liberate from sin, both public and private, asserting the claims of His Kingdom against all that militates against it. This commitment will also lead us to minister compassionately in His name to the imprisoned, the needy, and the oppressed.

Social concern is where the central issue of holiness – love – meets the road! If the heart of holiness is centered in loving "with all thy mind and thy neighbor as thyself," then holiness is inextricably linked to the way one treats his neighbor.

NEVER, NEVER, NEVER, NEVER!

by Larry D. Smith

"When the Spirit of God has been generated in a human being, it must not be shut up in the prayer meeting or church building, but turned on the saloons, the gambling houses, the haunts of shame." This vigorous call to evangelical social witness was issued in 1897 to the Women's Christian Temperance Union by its president, the indomitable Frances E. Willard. Over a century later, it remains a vigorous call to us.

As historian Jean Miller Schmidt explains, Willard "had consecrated herself completely to God during holiness meetings led by Phoebe Palmer and her husband Walter." She loved prayer meetings and church buildings, to be sure, for they were foundational to that warmhearted piety that must shape all godly character. But, as she also insisted, that piety could never be confined to religious structures, for, enflamed by the Spirit, its inevitable thrust was through the walls to Christianize the culture.

This is why Frances Willard joined thousands of others in a vast crusade to bring Christ's law to America's social fabric, Christ's mercy to its degraded masses, and Christ's judgment to its cesspools of evil—"the saloons, the gambling houses, the haunts of shame." After all, she was a devout Methodist, and like so many Methodists in that vast crusade, she was committed to her church's originating mission "to reform the continent and spread scriptural holiness over these lands." Stated thus in twofold form, that mission is really only one, for as we have always said, holiness in the sanctuary must become holiness in the public square.

SOCIAL WITNESS AFFIRMED

All this is affirmed in Article IX of the "Call to the Conservative Holiness Movement." Its authors are emphatic that the command of Jesus "to take up the cross and follow Him is a call to Christian social witness, for everywhere the Master went He ministered to both the spiritual and physical needs of people." Thus, the first dimension of this vital ministry is positive—doing what is right, reaching out "compassionately to the sick, the suffering and the forsaken." In contrast, the second dimension of Christian social witness, also defined in the "Call," is negative, opposing what is wrong, impelled "to resist courageously societal structures that oppose divine purpose and degrade human dignity."

As we obey Christ's command, therefore, inspired by His example, we are summoned, first, to *compassionate philanthropy*, and second, to *uncompromising protest.* One of the "Call's" most memorable statements is from Dr. Leon Hynson who puts this all in clear perspective. "Wherever the Christian lives an authentic life," he writes, "the world around is permeated with God's presence ... [He] raises the quality of life, makes social justice, equity, and integrity work. The pure in heart not only 'see' God but become the letters through which society sees Him."

"Faith working by love," Galatians 5:6, is the "theological formulation and foundation of Christian ethics," as Hynson continues to explain, as well as "the recurrent paradigm" of societal ministry in the Wesleyan tradition. This faith anchored securely in Christ's saving work brings us to personal salvation. But as it expresses itself thereafter in self-giving love, it becomes "intensely social," prompting us to follow Jesus "out into the world where economic slaveries, human indignity and oppression, poverty and disease, hold persons under purgations more severe than most of us are able to conceive."

SOCIAL WITNESS NEGLECTED

"Faith working by love" compels us, therefore, to challenge these hideous bastions of evil and to bring release in Christ to those imprisoned by them. At least, this is our respected historical position, though not always our consistent practice. For as Article IX asserts, "we have sometimes withdrawn into the cloistered walls of a narrow and narcissistic piety," centered in our own spiritual experience but divorced from the nastiness that lurks just outside those walls. "But this was not the pattern of our spiritual forebears who raised Christian consciousness in all the forums of public life and who filled their land with works of grace and mercy."

John Wesley was convinced that Christ's love was "the medicine of life," transforming rebellious sinners into robust saints. But as he also taught this same love was "the never-failing remedy for all the evils of a disordered world." With what appeared to be "a foolhardy courage worthy of Jack the Giant Killer," he set out determined to apply that medicine everywhere to heal the unspeakable horrors of English culture.

> Thus, as historian Earle E. Cairns has noted, Wesley "gave 30,000 [pounds] during his life to other people. In 1746 he opened the first free dispensary in England for medical aid to the poor of Bristol. ... He opened a Friends Society in 1785 to aid strangers in

> want. He wrote pamphlets against Methodists taking bribes for their vote, engaging in smuggling or swearing. He supported attempts at elementary education and the rise of Sunday schools. He opposed the slave trade and threw the support of the Methodists behind every effort to destroy it. His last letter was written to Wilberforce to encourage him in the fight against this trade which he called that 'execrable sum of all villainies.' He visited those in prison and encouraged John Howard in his work in prison reform."

Methodists and other "holiness people," who regarded themselves as Wesley's followers, committed themselves to his example. Nazarene scholar Dr. Timothy L. Smith documents how they united relentlessly with other evangelical Christians "to purge human society of all its ills [and] usher in Christ's reign on earth." In the greatest moral struggle of their times they rallied in a ferocious assault on slavery—an assault that shaped the origin of both the Wesleyan Methodist and the Free Methodist denominations. Later they threw themselves into the fight against the "demon rum," determined to "sweep away intemperance from the land," as one of their battle songs declared.

Nor was this all, for they entered the lists against ignorance, poverty, gambling, racism, economic inequity, political corruption, abortion and sexual degradation. They operated rescue missions, established orphanages, and scrubbed and saved the "soiled doves" exploited by Victorian America. C.T. Studd didn't call himself a Wesleyan, but his famous lines sum up the fiery dynamic of our tradition. *"Some wish to live within the sound of church or chapel bell; I want to run a rescue shop within a yard of hell."*

But then "in the early 20th century," as I have written before in these pages, came the "Great Reversal," as George Marsden calls it, "when all progressive social concern, became suspect among revivalist evangelicals and was relegated to a very minor role." This came primarily, as he believes, "in reaction to the Liberal Social Gospel," which had come to dominate mainline Protestantism.

"We never completely abandoned our heritage of Wesleyan social activism, but we certainly tempered our enthusiasm for it. Melvin Dieter thinks this came because we allowed our 'pietism to overcome [our] Wesleyan perfectionism,' while Donald Dayton links our waning social activism to the loss of the old postmillennial optimism that activated reformers to prepare a kingdom for their King. Whatever its causes, we may agree that the 'Great Reversal' is really the 'Great Betrayal' of 'scriptural holiness,' as we have always understood it. As our forebears would have asked, 'How can "faith working by love" turn away from a world of empty bellies and shattered dreams?'"

SOCIAL WITNESS RECLAIMED

At every point, the "Call" is firmly conservative, urging us to be who we really are. This demands that we recover the riches of our past in order to invest them in the destiny of our tomorrow: first in reverent service to our God, and second, in relevant service to our world. Thus, Article IX calls us to "renewed commitment to Christian social witness," emphasizing again its essential dimensions, *compassionate philanthropy*—ministering in Christ's name "to the imprisoned, the needy, and the oppressed," and *uncompromising protest*—asserting the claims of His Kingdom "against all that militates against it." Granted, there are many in the CHM who are doing both of these, but what we need so desperately as a movement is to reclaim the throbbing passion that once sent us out everywhere to

Christianize our culture. If we are to do this—and God grant that we shall—we must respond firmly to these imperatives:

Renewed hope. It's time to stop wringing our hands over the miseries of our time and determine by God's grace to do something about them. Our hope in Christ transcends the present evil and impels us to extend His hands to touch the hopeless. Church history shows that social wrong has often been far worse than it is today, but that faithful Christians, determined to be "salt and light," have turned back the tide. With God's help, we can do this again! After all, we serve God who promises to lift up His banner against the foe and fight beside us. So throw yourself now into the struggle. "All that is necessary for evil to triumph," warned Edmund Burke, "is for good men to do nothing."

Personal Piety. Social activism can never be an end in itself, but rather an essential by-product of deep Christian devotion, marked by faith, love and obedience, and nourished by prayer, Scripture and the other means of grace. This brings a winsome and courageous love that is a powerful influence for righteousness. Remember, too, that your local church is a frontline battle station that you must strengthen and support in this great struggle against the darkness. For all of us, then, it's first to the altar in worship, then to the sidewalk in witness!

Active Involvement. Each of us in our little corner must light a candle to disperse the darkness, and those little flames flickering together will become a radiant light bringing cheer, hope and renewal. Make up your mind to lift your candle now. Write a check to support a home for unwed mothers; volunteer to tutor a Mexican boy struggling with English grammar; join the neighborhood improvement association; reach out to a frightened unwed mother; help out in the local food pantry; become a police chaplain or a hospital aide. Write a letter to the newspaper;, sign a petition; run for the local school board; let your Congressman know that you're for marriage as the Bible defines it.

Cautious Networking. In the social crisis now confronting us we must determine, as did John Wesley, to form a "league offensive and defensive with every soldier of Christ." This means reaching out to other Christians to do what we never could do alone. Granted, this demands cautious participation and determined purpose never to compromise our own distinctive principles. But there are all kinds of advocacy groups that we can support and even join in the struggle for right and against evil—abortion protests, political rallies, ministerial associations. Think, too, of Habitat for Humanity, the Salvation Army, World Hope International, the WCTU, and the Voice of the Martyrs.

Fierce Determination. Remember Wilberforce's lifetime thrown into the battle against slavery, Amy Carmichael's struggle in India to save little girls from forced prostitution, or Francis Willard's assault on whiskey and the mistreatment of women. They were effective because they were Christians who simply would never quit. Jesus has all the ages to consummate His purpose, and in each of them we must be faithful, refusing to "grow weary in well doing." It was in 1941 during the agonies of World War II that Winston Churchill charged the students at Harrow, "Never give in—never, never, never, never!"

This must also be our resolve. Give in? "Never, never, never, never!" For as Frances Willard insisted, holiness in the sanctuary must become holiness in the public square. Yes, it's time for another great crusade to bring Christ's law to America's social fabric, Christ's mercy to its degraded masses, and Christ's judgment to its cesspools of evil—"the saloons, the gambling houses, the haunts of shame."

HOLINESS AND SOCIAL CONCERN

by Michael R. Avery

Today over a billion people in the world live on less than a dollar a day. That means over a billion men and women face a daily struggle to find food, water and shelter with less money than you would spend for an order of fries or your favorite donut.

More than 24,000 children die every day from preventable causes like diarrhea (contracted from unclean water); while more than 16,000 die from starvation.

The average American finds it hard to grasp this kind of poverty. Especially since the hardest struggle many face in their daily routine is fastening their pants. Yet not all Americans are blessed by being average. More than 16 million children live in households that struggle to put food on the table. There are almost 14 million single parents (84% single moms) endeavoring to raise 26% of America's children, and half of them live in poverty.

Over one third of America's elderly live below the poverty line. Thousands of panhandlers and homeless people beg on the street corners and sleep over the warm grates of every major city.

Multiplied thousands of the working poor have homes in need of repair or cars in need of maintenance that can't and won't be fixed because there is neither the money to have it done nor the skill to do it themselves. Many of these folks sit in a pew next to you.

SHOULD THIS REALLY BOTHER ME?

Bob Pierce often prayed, "Let my heart be broken by the things that break the heart of God." All serious Christians pray this prayer. They also go further. They strive to learn what breaks the heart of God and then act on what they learn. Fortunately for us, God's view on the subject is not hidden. In the laws given to the developing nation of Israel, He addresses every segment of society that needs to hear a voice of compassion: the widows, orphans, strangers (aliens), the injured, the hungry, women, those who have been enslaved by debt, the marginalized, the disenfranchised, and others who are oppressed or disadvantaged in some other way (Leviticus and Deuteronomy).

He makes it clear that honoring these laws is so close to His heart that the Jewish nation's peaceful and continuing existence in the land is conditioned on obedience to these laws (Jeremiah 7:5-7). The prophet Amos gives us a glimpse into both God's attitude toward and His judgment upon those who ignore justice for the distressed and exploit the poor.

The New Testament speaks loudly on behalf of this same group of people. Jesus communicated His concerns powerfully through such accounts as The Rich Man and Lazarus (Luke 16:19-31), The Rich Young Ruler (Mark 10:17-22), The Good Samaritan (Luke 10:25-37), and The Sheep and Goats (Matt. 25: 31-46). The newly formed Church appointed a group of deacons just to care for the widows (Acts 6). When the Jerusalem Council gave Paul and Barnabas the right hand of fellowship and commissioned them to go to the Gentiles, it was with the admonition to "remember the poor" (Gal. 2:10).

The Apostle John, who may have known the heart of Jesus better than any other, spoke these words, "But whoso hath this world's good, and seeth his brother have need, and shutteth up his bowels of compassion from him, how dwelleth the love of God in him?" (1 John 3:17). James tells us that pure religion and true faith are validated by how we respond to those in need (James 1:27, 2:15-17).

"THERE IS NO HOLINESS BUT SOCIAL HOLINESS"

The above quotation is not from John Wesley but from Mike Avery! Yes, Wesley made that statement, but he was not referring to social action but rather to people whose holiness led them to separate themselves from the body of Christ. We would call that "Lone Ranger religion." I am referring to social concern and action. Why? Because social concern is where the central issue of holiness—love —meets the road! If the heart of holiness is centered in loving "with all thy mind and thy neighbor as thyself," then holiness is inextricably linked to the way one treats his neighbor. It seems to me to be quite impossible to claim a heart full of love for God yet offer a hand empty of compassion toward my neighbor. Dag Hammarskjold was correct in saying that the road to holiness passes through the world of action (1 John 3:17).

CALLING THE CHM TO SOCIAL CONCERN!

Article IX of the "Call to the Conservative Holiness Movement" states that the CHM to a great degree has turned its gaze away from society's neediest people toward the "cloistered walls of a narrow and narcissistic piety." It further states that by doing so the CHM has forsaken the pattern of her spiritual forefathers who not only declared the gospel verbally but demonstrated it visibly by building orphanages, establishing homes for unwed mothers, and planting Gospel missions on every skid row in every large city of America. To them taking the gospel to the "least of these my brethren" was the only way to fulfill the command to "preach the gospel to every creature."

HAS THE CHM FAILED?

It is not as easy as it might seem to evaluate the extent to which the present day conservative holiness churches are engaged in social action ministries in their local communities. There are many cases in which individuals are involved in volunteer work, give significantly to fund these types of ministries, or directly assist individuals who are needy, though the CHM church itself has no formal participation in any social ministry. For example, I found a situation in which two men are supporting a single mom and her two children: providing housing, Christian school tuition, a vehicle to get her to work, etc. Since this is not a structured ministry, it would not show up in a list of such ministries operated by a church. Nevertheless it is the very kind of social action that the Bible addresses and clearly reflects a passion for social concern. I am hopeful that this example is a norm rather than an exception.

I found a few cases in which a church chose to give a small amount of financial support to organizations that specialize in some particular area of ministry to the needy rather than directly engage in these ministries themselves. Organizations like Love and Hope in Action, The Salvation Army, regional food banks, Habitat for Humanity, city missions, Christian clearing houses, and a host of others specialize in social outreach and do a good job on the local level.

The question remains as to the movement at large. Is the CHM failing in the area of social concern as a whole? The only way I had to find an answer to this question was a less than perfect method of just looking at the number of actual ministries operated and funded by conservative holiness churches. I did not include ministries that were federally or state-funded with the exception of food banks. Out of approximately 3,000 churches identified as CHM churches I was able to locate five prison/jail ministries, three rescue missions, six food distribution ministries, two free clothing ministries, and one home for unwed mothers. I am quite sure there are other churches with ministries that I did not discover. Nevertheless, even if the numbers above were doubled or tripled, the ratio of ministries to churches would still be quite small. I will let my readers draw their own conclusions.

I also contacted world mission organizations that identify with the CHM to see what they were doing to provide care for orphans, clean water for villages, medical care for the destitute, and food for the hungry. According to *Rope Holders* (missions newsletter) there are approximately 31 organizations that serve the CHM as foreign mission agencies. We were able to get responses from 29. With the one exception of work among Native Americans, all responses involved work outside the US. The table below shows the percentage that answered in the affirmative to various categories of social ministry:

Care for orphans	17%
Food provided daily	27%
Education for the poor	48%
Clean water	20%
Medical clinic	20%
Medicine for preventable causes	34%

What is being done by *individuals* within the CHM is being done, as it should be, without knowledge to others, so there is no way to draw any valid conclusions. If you look at what the CHM is doing *organizationally* in America and overseas, one can draw his own conclusions. However, there is one conclusion that can be drawn that may not be as obvious as others but needs to be pointed out nonetheless. The CHM has clearly lost the full measure of the social conscience that gripped our forefathers. Our Methodist holiness forefathers filled their cities and towns with acts of mercy. It is estimated that John Wesley gave over 30,000 pounds (over $4,000,000 in today's value) to other people during his life. He opened the first free dispensary in England for medical aid to the poor. He organized a society to aid strangers in need. He supported education for the poor, opposed the slave trade, and encouraged prison reform.

Succeeding Methodists battled slavery, alcohol, ignorance, poverty, gambling, racism, political corruption, abortion and sexual degradation. Phoebe Palmer, known for the Tuesday Meeting for the Promotion of Holiness, may have done some of her best work through her Five Points Mission. Many of the Nazarene and the Pilgrim Holiness churches had their origins as rescue missions. Many, if not most, of the early Bible schools located in large cities so they would be near those who needed help in both soul and body. Martin Wells Knapp pushed God's Bible School to the forefront of the "soup, soap, and salvation" work in Cincinnati. Lela McConnell saw the need outside the cities and carried the same passion for acts of mercy to the Appalachian poor in the mountains of Eastern Kentucky. As Larry Smith would say in reference to our history, "We Wesleyans have punched holes in the darkness."

REASONS OR EXCUSES?

It would be simplistic and irresponsible not to acknowledge the many problems associated with undertaking many of these ministries. For example, the regulatory role of government through federal and state agencies has made it next to impossible for small denominations or churches to operate any type of facility for those who need both Christian compassion and professional care.

Furthermore, government's involvement in the whole arena of care for the needy has created such a "welfare culture" that, for many individuals, it has taken the heart out of helping the less fortunate. Many are turned off by a generation of poor who not only expect help but demand it. However, this is not sufficient reason to face our communities with a closed fist.

There is also a very real danger that we allow social concern to become an end in itself. Our attempts to help society will not make a society with better men. It is the power of the gospel that changes hearts, thereby making better men who will in turn make better societies. On the occasion of William Booth's 80th birthday, he wrote to his officers these words, "But while you strive to deliver them from their temporal distresses, and endeavor to rescue them from the causes that have led to their unfortunate condition, you must seek, above all, to turn their miseries to good account by making them help the salvation of their souls and their deliverance from the wrath to come. It will be a very small reward for all your toils if, after bringing them into a condition of wellbeing here, they perish hereafter."

Many have sought to alleviate the sufferings of someone in need, only to find they had been duped by a professional con artist. I truly understand this dilemma. Since I travel a lot, I am often asked for help with fuel when I stop at a service station. Of course I am skeptical, but since I have no way of knowing if the need is real or not, I often help by putting fuel in the tank of those professing need, never money in their pocket. I do not believe we should foolishly give money away or subsidize laziness, addictions or sin. But I believe it is better to help a hundred fakes than to close my heart to humanity and end up failing to help the one truly in need.

You may excuse yourself from helping others by claiming you can't find any real needs or that you are too poor yourself to help someone else. You may not feel wealthy or think you are, but if you have running water, a shelter over your head, clothes to wear, food to eat, and some means of transportation (public or private), you are in the top 15 percent of the world's people of wealth. It has been my experience that those with less means are generally more willing to help than those with great means. The same is true with churches. Generosity is not controlled by one's bank account but by one's heart! Rich churches who neglect the poor are not the communities of God, just as rich people who neglect the poor are not the people of God!

WHAT CAN WE DO?

First, start with becoming a Christian who takes the Bible seriously! Our lives should be a living witness against a worldly church that has become self-satisfied with its affluence and privileged position. We should be a living reproach to the nominal Christian who cares more about the number of shopping days left until Christmas than he does about the poor. We should simplify our lives so that we can share with those who truly need our help both in our own community and around the world!

Second, care enough to be informed. Educate yourself about global issues such as preventable disease, clean water, hunger, sex trafficking, the plight of the unborn and education. Find out what is happening in your own sphere of influence and do something about it. Commit to practicing the law of love. Develop a systematic approach to helping others that follows the Biblical admonition to care first for one's own family (1 Tim 5:8), then fellow believers (Gal. 6:10), and then to every human being possible (Gal. 6:10; James 1:27, 2:26; cf. Rom. 13:1-10).

Third, give your financial support systematically and thoughtfully, not just emotionally. It should be noted that the early church used great care in discerning who should receive their support. For example, a widow was to be put on a list for permanent, lifetime support only if she met certain criteria. Paul sets these down clearly in 1 Timothy 5:3-10, insisting that she must be at least 60 years old, "left alone" without family or presumably any other means of support, a woman of prayer, married only once, and having a reputation for good works, among other things. In contrast, Paul admonishes the Thessalonians to withhold their social care to those unwilling but able to work, remarking, "If anyone will not work, neither let him eat" (2 Thess. 3:6-15). Giving should always be done in a way that doesn't support bad behavior or subsidize addictive habits or close the door for the Gospel. Give wisely but give. This also includes being wise in your giving to mission organizations and agencies that care for orphans and feed the hungry. Do some investigation into any organization that you plan to support. Ask for a public audit or go online and read the audit. Ask how much of your money actually goes to the need and how much stays in the local office for administrative overhead. If no answer is forthcoming, find another organization that will give answers. Legitimate ministries are more than willing to share any information that will help you give confidently and generously.

Fourth, pray. The giving of your time and treasure may be small but the offering up of your prayers can be large! We cannot take up every kind of injustice or concern in the world—to even try to do so would do us in. But we can enter the arena of social concern on the wings of prayer. Prayer is necessary if the forces of darkness and the demonic principalities that are behind the institutional structures that are responsible for so much poverty and suffering are to be defeated.

Everett Hale said, "I am only one, but still I am one. I cannot do everything, but still I can do something; and because I cannot do everything, I will not refuse to do the something that I can do."

I cannot cut the ropes that bind the little girls of Thailand as they wait to be sold to some vile monster; but I can pressure my government to get involved, support the organizations that do, and be faithful in my prayers to defeat the demonic forces that hold this corrupt system in place. I can't save every child that dies in the Sudan, but I can support a missionary who braves the risk of working there. I can't alleviate all the suffering in Cincinnati or even all that is found on the street where I live, but there are some things I can and must do! I will probably never feel that what I did was quite enough, even though it was my best. I may always feel a little skeptical as to whether the ones I reached out to really needed my help or truly appreciated my efforts. But I am always comforted and motivated by these words, "Inasmuch as ye have done it unto one of the least of these my brethren, ye have done it unto me" (Matt. 25:40).

Chapter 10

A CALL TO RESURGENT HOPE

We call our movement to the joyous expectation of victory which so motivated our spiritual forebears to claim the American frontier for Jesus Christ.

The past must serve as a guidepost, not a hitching post. It should be the rudder on the ship, not the anchor. God consistently reveals Himself as One who is forward-looking. He is primarily interested in where we are going, not where we have been.

RENEWING THE VISION

by Michael R. Avery

Charles C. McCabe was the Director of Church Extension for the Methodist Episcopal Church, as well as a brilliant strategist. In the spring of 1881, he was riding a train in the Pacific Northwest when he saw an article about the National Convention of the Free Thinkers of America. The newspaper included the text of a speech delivered by prominent atheist Robert Ingersoll. As McCabe read the speech he became quite angry. Ingersoll had said, "The churches are dying out all across America. They are struck with death! By the dawn of the 20th century, churches will be but relics of a bygone day."

McCabe got off the train and fired off a telegram to Mr. Ingersoll in Chicago. It read, "Dear Bob, We are building more than one church a day for every day of the year and propose to make it two a day!" The story got out, and someone composed the following chorus:

The infidels, a motley band, in council met and said,
"The churches die throughout the land, the last will soon be dead."

When suddenly a message came that filled them with dismay,
"All hail the power of Jesus' name, we're building two a day."

"We're building two a day, dear Bob; we're building two a day!
"All hail the power of Jesus' name, we're building two a day!"

Charles McCabe clearly shared the vision of John Wesley, Methodism's founder, "to reform the continent and to spread scriptural holiness across these lands." Methodism envisioned itself as a reform movement. This vision propelled the Methodist Church to the forefront of outreach and pioneer evangelism in America until it could be said that the Methodists owned the 19th century!

Despite the multitude of stories telling of the Church's transformative impact on cities, countries and civilizations, there has been no shortage of hostile voices predicting her demise. Yet even while the scoffers scoff, the Church of Jesus Christ steadily penetrates a darkened world like yeast penetrates a loaf of bread "until the whole be leavened." It will continue to do so until that day when "at the name of Jesus every knee shall bow, of things in heaven, and things in earth, and things under the earth; And every tongue will confess that Jesus Christ is Lord, to the glory of God the Father." The future of the Church does not hang in the balance! Victory for the Church of Jesus Christ is inevitable!

The truth in the paragraph above stands without equivocation. However, any thinking person who reads the above statement and then simply looks at what is happening in the vast majority of churches in North America and Europe today would have cause to question the veracity of what I wrote. It is true that the Invisible Church of Jesus Christ is and will be triumphant. But it is not true that every part of the visible church on earth experiences that same conquering spirit. While the Church is harvesting a bumper crop in Asia, Latin America and Africa, the harvest seems to be rotting in the field in Europe and North America.

The problem is certainly not with the Lord of the Church or with His power to prevail. The problem lies with a Laodicean spirit that has gripped the visible church of North America and Europe. The problem is not new! Read Paul's words to a church that was not yet twenty-five years old! Take a moment to read again the first three chapters of the book of The Revelation. Take a literary walk down the pages of church history, reading the stories of the reformers and the revivalists, and you will see what I mean!

A willingness to acknowledge historical fact and present reality about certain parts of the Church should not turn us into pessimists. One does not have to join the "Church is dead" movement to be able to admit that the visible Church has at times lost her way, backslidden, become unfruitful, and needed major reformation and revival. As a matter of fact, I believe the Church in America is in such a time right now. James MacDonald says the evangelical church is experiencing a time of "epic failure." He further says, "Until we acknowledge that the church in North America is failing, we won't take the steps necessary to see that trend reversed." MacDonald's word to the evangelical Church should be taken to heart by the Conservative Holiness Movement as well.

A CALL TO RESURGENT HOPE

Along with the faculty of God's Bible School and College, I have the greatest appreciation for, and the deepest commitment to, that part of God's Church identified as the Conservative Holiness Movement. This is the tradition that GBS has lived and worked within long before there was such a name designation or a movement identified as such. The "Call to the Conservative Holiness Movement" was written by our faculty as an attempt to restate the strengths of that tradition, to acknowledge its weaknesses, and to dialogue on how to restore what is vital to its future. By the very nature of such a call, we are acknowledging problems, struggling to find answers, and humbly offering solutions.

The last section, Article X, in the "Call to the Conservative Holiness Movement" is "A Call to Resurgent Hope." The CHM needs a renewed vision for its future. It lacks a "grand idea" to marshal its youth and to propel it forward. The absence of such a vision has caused the movement to become disoriented and allowed it to drift away from its historical landmarks—the things that made it special in the first place. However, the key to a renewed vision or a new vision altogether begins with a willingness to acknowledge apparent problems with an eye to corrective measures.

AN ELEPHANT IN THE ROOM!

It has been obvious for a long time to many of the leaders within the CHM that the movement is in a state of serious decline. It has failed to grow numerically by means of new conversions, while membership rolls in some of the largest and oldest denominations have decreased as much as 60%. Unfortunately too many key leaders have simply ignored the obvious. You could say it is "the elephant in the room" that nobody wants to talk about!

To reinforce my own observations with facts, I had a third-party survey conducted. The survey was conducted among the eighteen denominations that identify with the CHM. The leadership of each denomination was asked to identify its top two churches so that the pastor of these churches could be interviewed. (It should be pointed out that using the top churches in each group heavily weighted the survey towards a more favorable outcome.) Fifteen of the groups cooperated with the survey, which allowed us to question the pastors of 30 of the top churches in these denominational groups. I then surveyed four of the largest independent churches in the CHM and added the results to this survey.

The pastors were asked three questions: (1) How many conversions of unchurched people have you had in the last five years that have been discipled to the level of membership (not yet a member but ready to be)? (2) How many conversions of unchurched people have you had in the last five years that have been discipled to the level of maturity that allows them to be involved in ministry? (3) How many third-generation Christians do you have in your church?

What We Found:

1. Eighty percent of the top churches in the CHM have had no unchurched person converted and discipled to the level of membership within the last five years.
2. In the six largest churches surveyed, only one had unchurched people converted and discipled to the level of membership in the last five years. Only two had converts discipled to the point of ministry involvement.
3. The churches with the most third-generation Christians tended to have the least number of unchurched converts, while churches with the least number of third generation Christians tended to have the most unchurched converts.
4. The majority of the churches surveyed had at least one convert that had been discipled enough to use in ministry but was still unable to be considered for membership.
5. There were three churches that I considered "outliers" and set them apart in the survey results. Together these three churches had 180 converts of unchurched people in the last five years. Sixty of these converts were discipled to the level of membership. One hundred

twenty of these converts were discipled to the level of ministry. All three churches had a combined total of only 24 third-generation Christians (that is an average of only eight each). These churches are exceptional and have something to teach us!

This survey highlights a number of problems. First, most CHM churches are not reaching the unchurched. Second, when a CHM church does see unchurched people converted it rarely retains these converts. This problem of attrition has several contributing causes, but it is primarily because the average CHM church has failed to address the process necessary to grow these converts and to assimilate them into the core fellowship of the church (the process of becoming and belonging). Hence, most of them backslide or go to another church. Third, the survey revealed something else that I had only surmised. It revealed that churches with high numbers of third-generation Christians do the poorest job of reaching the unchurched. This is true despite the fact that many of these operate impressive ministries to that very population. It is alarming to see that these large churches that are resource rich can operate impressive outreach ministries and never truly "reach out."

This is the elephant in the room!

HOW DO YOU EAT AN ELEPHANT?

Occasionally one of my colleagues or students will share with me what seems to them to be an insurmountable problem. I will listen carefully, then ask them this question, "How do you eat an elephant?" While they are looking at me in absolute bewilderment, I will answer for them, "One bite at a time!" All of our problems, no matter how large, can and must be addressed "one bite at a time." For the CHM, the process of addressing the serious problem of decline will be a long-term deliberate strategy that must be implemented "one bite at a time."

Success in eating the elephant means that the CHM must avoid the danger of two extremes. The first extreme is to do nothing. Since the elephant is so big and the challenge is so overwhelming, the danger is that we just ignore it and do nothing at all. On the other hand, we must avoid the other extreme of trying to eat the elephant in just a few bites. Massive and sudden change can divide, demoralize, and possibly destroy a church or movement.

DOING NOTHING IS NOT ACCEPTABLE!

However insurmountable the problem may appear, to be doing nothing is not an option. Like a man paddling across the Atlantic with a hole in his boat, we can neglect the problems of our movement for a while, but if they are not eventually addressed we will certainly sink. Complacency can be one of our biggest enemies. It is sometimes hard to spot complacency because it can hide its failure to act behind impressive rationalization.

Complacent leaders and pastors will pose the argument that true success cannot be measured or quantified. They say that such measurements are the world's way of evaluating a successful ministry and that simply counting conversions, members, offerings, buildings, etc., is not the way God measures success. They contend that the only true criterion for ministry is faithfulness. There is so much truth in this argument that it is difficult to debate. There is much to be said from the Word and from practical ministry about faithfulness. It is extremely important in both the eyes of God and men.

However, holding up faithfulness as the final measure of true success can be a "cop out" for failing to do the hard work of reaching people. Even if that isn't the case, it is certainly an oversimplification. I agree with Timothy Keller when he says that there is another Biblical gauge for evaluating ministry beyond basing success mostly on *faithfulness*. That gauge is *fruitfulness* (John 15:8)!

If complacent leaders and lay members can comfort themselves with an appeal to their faithfulness (one that has certainly been uncoupled from the concept of fruitfulness), then that may prove to be a strong enough "sleeping potion" to keep them from addressing the true barrenness of their particular denominations and churches. I am afraid that as long as the various groups that make up the CHM can afford to hold the annual IHC, operate their annual camp meetings, and give respectable offerings to a foreign missions program, they will remain complacent—even accepting—toward the failure of the local church to be fruitful and reach its surrounding community.

THE IMPORTANCE OF VISION RENEWAL

If you have ever driven a car with misaligned wheels, you know that it is difficult to keep the car in the middle of your lane, for it constantly wants to pull to one side. That is what it is like to be in a movement, church or organization that lacks vision. People may be very busy doing something, but they are continuously pulled off center, away from the main thing. Without a compelling vision to motivate, energize and direct, they will wear themselves out with meaningless activity. Any church or movement that is engaged in such activity becomes the breeding ground for skepticism, criticism and a host of "rabbit trails" that take it away from its main objective.

In greyhound racing there is a little mechanical rabbit covered in fur that sits on the end of a long metal rod that circles the track ahead of the dogs. The operator of this mechanical rabbit always keeps the rabbit ahead of the dogs so as to keep them running but never allowing them to catch it. In one race, while the dogs were hotly pursuing the rabbit, there was a short in the electrical system that caused the rabbit to explode. With no rabbit to chase, the dogs didn't know what to do. Some of them went crazy jumping through the fence. Others just wandered aimlessly around the track. Still others laid down on the track and howled at the spectators. Not one dog finished the race. Without a vision to pursue, dreams fade, people drift, and once vibrant movements slowly die.

VISION OBSTACLES

The CHM is resource rich! It has a wealth of talented people who are deeply committed to their faith. It possesses what it takes to move forward with the work of vision discovery, renewal and implementation. Yet it does have some major "vision obstacles" that will have to be overcome. These include the following:

Reluctant Leadership. So much rises and falls around leadership. The CHM struggles to be open to the kind of visionary leader that has the capacity to lead it from where it is to where it needs to go. Even where that kind of leadership exists, it has too often bowed to the politics of fear or lacked the resolve to push beyond the obstacles.

Pietistic Pride. The CHM battles with a strange paradox. On the one hand, it struggles with an inferiority complex; while on the other hand, it struggles with pietistic pride. There are times when our opinion of ourselves is too exalted—so much so, indeed, that we tend to look down on the rest of Christ's body as "not quite where we are." This sanctimonious arrogance needs to be replaced with a little sanctified humility. After all, pride made the Devil the Devil!

Preoccupation with the Past. When CHM folks get together you will hear far more talk about our "holiness heritage" than you ever will about our "holiness future." Our Methodist Holiness history is fascinating! But it is still history! The past must serve as a guidepost, not a hitching post. It should be the rudder on the ship, not the anchor. God consistently reveals Himself as One who is forward-looking. He is primarily interested in where we are going, not where we have been. It is the Devil who wants us preoccupied with the past! Movements and churches that have been mightily used of God in the past and for one reason or the other get stuck there will be set aside and someone else or something else will be raised up to take their place.

Resistance to Change. Continual change is the reality of our time. The church is not an isolated island from the rest of society, and by its very nature it cannot be. It, too, is changing. As a matter of fact, change is not new to the Church. For those of us within the holiness tradition, John Wesley and the early Methodists serve as an example of innovative and creative change to meet the ministry needs of their time. The CHM has proven quite resistant to change in methodology, technology and organizational structure, even when it is apparent that change could advance the kingdom without any compromise to the message.

An Unhealthy Focus on Single Issues. Churches were never meant to have a single focus like Pizza Hut or Jiffy Lube. The Church must be fully Biblical and properly balanced in all its priorities and emphases! To be a healthy body, it must be a whole body. Too many CHM churches are known for one thing, and that is the lifestyle positions they embrace. When this single focus prevails, it can hurt the church both internally and externally. Biblical holiness does in fact have behavioral consequences that impact my lifestyle. But it also casts them as a part of discipleship and growth where they are lived out in an atmosphere of relaxed self-discipline and humble dependence on God, never as the main thing.

Fear-Driven Decision Making. Movements, churches, and pastors who constantly test the winds of "what others might think" end up neurotic, paranoid and pathetically immobile. Fear has been the catalyst for many needless rules and regulations. The fear of what others "might think" has killed many positive outreach initiatives. A man-fearing spirit and the general fear of change have hindered churches from needed adjustments that would have positioned them to better serve their own people as well as those they might reach.

VISION BEGINS WITH GOD!

God is more than willing to help a struggling or failing church or movement to regain its footing, but He will not climb over the impediments of no vision, poor planning, weak execution, horizontal thinking and a lack of faith. Leadership must take seriously the work of vision casting.

For me to propose a vision or even attempt to restate a vision for the churches, the denominations, and the organizations that make up the 21st century CHM would push the boundaries of arrogance or ignorance (I will let you decide). The work of vision-casting and mission development is not a "cut and paste" moment achieved by a few hours of "googling" all the good web sites.

Vision comes from the Lord! It comes when leaders and laymen seek God, find a divine burden, and mold it to their situation! Vision is not some mystical dream detached from reality. Whatever vision God gives a church, it will have some parallel to the mission and vision laid out for us in the book of Acts and duplicated throughout the centuries by the Church. Vision is anchored in one's core values, grows out of one's main reason for existence, and fits perfectly within the context of one's ministry situation (gifts and resources).

Vision is birthed when someone has a heart that aches so badly to know how to advance God's Kingdom that he or she is willing to get alone with God long enough to say, "Speak, Lord, for your servant heareth," and then stay still long enough for God to speak to the situation. Vision is not solely owned or produced by one person, but I do believe that God normally puts the vision for a church, an organization or a movement into the heart of one person and not a group of people. I also believe that He confirms and refines that vision as the leader shares it with a small group of elders or spiritual leaders to whom he is accountable or with whom he shares oversight of the ministry.

VISION COMPONENTS

A vision statement explains where a church or denomination is headed and helps to formulate a picture of what it will "look like" as it accomplishes its mission. I can't author a vision statement for the CHM or the individual churches that compose its membership, but if I could, the following components would be a central part of that statement.

UpReach. I believe prayer and worship are two core elements that are struggling to survive in ways that truly impact the CHM. We live in a post Christian culture where not only do men sin with no sense of remorse, but where anti-Biblical values and anti-Christian views are entrenched at the highest levels of the institutions that undergird and govern our society. Only prayer can break such a stronghold. We must once again become a praying church.

The culture we are called to win is one that is lonely, empty and materialistic. Men and women are desperately seeking for something they do not have—something transcendent. They are crushed by the disappointment that they cannot create happiness for themselves beyond the momentary. They have a deep longing in their souls to know, to experience and to worship God. The church that provides an experience of unashamed worship marked by the presence of God is the church that will never lack for people. We must return to the kind of worship that is marked by God's presence. This may be our greatest need!

OutReach. Many holiness churches began as storefront missions. They located where the sinners were because they believed it was their main job to see sinners saved, sanctified and established in the family of God. It seems that the CHM no longer believes that this is its main mission, and unfortunately the statistics support such a conclusion. The CHM has become primarily a preservation movement. However, that can change! A renewed vision for the CHM should make the Great Commission a vital part of its main mission so that we might "reform the nation and spread scriptural holiness across this land."

InReach. According to Dr. Brian Black, there are approximately 3,000 churches in the USA that in some way identify with the CHM. (Compare this to the North American church numbers for the Nazarenes, 4,800; the Wesleyans, 1,710; and the Free Methodists, 957.) With all these churches and all the individual talent within the CHM, one would think the movement could and should be doing something significant for the Kingdom of God.

However, we are resource rich and cooperation poor. We have miserably failed to reach within—to join hands and unite for the greater good of advancing the work of God in church planting, education, printing, missions and compassionate care. Instead of one or two strong mission organizations, there are thirty-one struggling ones. Instead of one or two strong colleges there are eight struggling ones. Instead of one strong holiness church in town there are four "family controlled" struggling ones. Cooperation for stewardship reasons alone would free up millions of dollars to further the Kingdom and the message of scriptural holiness! No movement on earth could gain more from just simply working together than could the CHM.

DownReach. The CHM has a wealth of Biblical, theological, doctrinal and practical teaching that is not being passed down to new Christians or to younger generations. The CHM needs a renewed commitment to discipleship, mentoring and preaching. Discipleship is the perfect arena to "teach" many things that should not and cannot be adequately "preached." Mentoring is the key to helping our immature converts and young people maneuver the choppy waters of life successfully. Just keeping the few converts we do have coupled with saving our own would double our population numbers within a few years.

Preaching, as it is being done in many CHM churches, is passionate exhortation with the goals of inspiration, motivation and evaluation. Preaching in today's world needs to be passionate explanation with the goal of transformation and application. Postmodern minds today don't want someone "yelling" at them. They want someone explaining the Bible and giving ways to apply it to life right now!

SOMEONE HAS GOT TO SEE IT!

Francis Asbury saw an American frontier evangelized for Christ, and the circuit rider was born. William Booth saw the poor of England sinking in despair, and the Salvation Army was born! Martin Wells Knapp saw a school to train a new generation of Christian soldiers, and God's Bible School was born. Rev. Eber Teter saw the state of Alabama without the message of heart holiness, and the Friendship Wesleyan Methodist Church was born—the church at whose altar I found saving grace. Someone must see what can be before it can or will come to pass!

The founder of Disney World, Walt Disney, died five years before Disney World was completed. On opening day in 1971 someone said to director Mike Vance, "Isn't it too bad Walt Disney didn't live to see this?" To which Vance replied, "Oh, Walt did see it! That's why it's here."

Somebody has got to dream and envision a renewed holiness movement. I long for a movement unified in purpose, linking arms together in mission and message! Martin Luther King saw an America where racial inequality was abolished. Remember how he explained that vision. "He (God) has allowed me to go up to the mountain. And I've looked over. And I've seen the Promised Land. I may not get there with you. But I want you to know tonight that we, as a people, will get to the Promised Land!"

I, too, have been to the mountain top, and I've seen the other side! The CHM just needs more mountain climbers who will get above the fog at ground level and see what "can be" in our tomorrows!

SO WHAT OF THE FUTURE?

by Larry D. Smith

"Wellington defeated ...." These words, according to unauthenticated reports, were flashed by signal flags from Winchester Cathedral, Monday, June 19, 1815, bringing England its first word from Waterloo. For near that town, about eight miles southeast of Brussels, Belgium, a French army under Napoleon Bonaparte had met the day before in ferocious combat with English forces and their allies commanded by Arthur, Duke of Wellington. His countrymen were gripped with almost unbearable suspense, for as they knew, that bloody battlefield would decide the fate of Europe.

At last, a sailing vessel brought eagerly awaited news. This was to be relayed to London by semaphoric code, beginning at Winchester, where high in the cathedral tower an operator began to arrange his flags to send the message. But unexpectedly a heavy fog descended to blot it out. All that anyone had been able to read were those two dreaded words, *"Wellington defeated ...."* Gloom filled the atmosphere. But then the fog lifted, and the operator was able to send his entire message: *"Wellington Defeated Napoleon at Waterloo."* Despair gave way to celebration.

So it is for us! Too often the message of Christian triumph is obscured by the devastating terrors that surround us. Then faith gives way to fear, and our faltering hearts are gripped with discouragement and dismay. Reports of betrayal and defeat leave us reeling with a sense of casualty and loss. Then suddenly the mists are lifted, and we see the full message of Christian triumph blazing out again in the enshrouding darkness.

This message centers "in the resplendent hope that we have through Christ's victory accomplished in His incarnation, atoning death, and resurrection," as Article X of the "Call to the Conservative Holiness Movement" so forcibly reminds us. "The sure and certain anchor of the soul, this hope has given gladness and assurance to faithful believers all throughout the centuries of the Church's struggle with the forces of entrenched evil. It assures us of present victory in our personal lives and corporate ministry, but it also points to the final triumph when every knee shall bow and every tongue shall confess that Jesus Christ is Lord."

So what of the future? United with Christ personally by faith and corporately in baptism, we are members of His Body, which is the Church. As such, we have no fear of its future, for He has promised that not even the gates of hell ever shall prevail against it. But as we also know, our Lord has made no such promise to the CHM or to any other movement or denomination that ever has arisen. Such groups often have emerged within the Church, sometimes with great enthusiasm, gradually drifted from their original mission and finally disappeared. That fine old English scholar Isaac Taylor once warned that "a moral wave measured eighty years—forty to reach its crest and break, and forty to subside and be lost."

Yet decline and disappearance are not inevitable—or at least, they can be greatly delayed—if we will remain faithful to the original vision that gave us origin and translate that vision into vigorous, relevant and creative ministry. Remember that God "raised us up" as a reform movement with the specific purpose to bring revival and renewal to both the Church and to the culture, commissioned specifically "to spread scriptural holiness over these lands."

This is the particular niche that He gives us still, our *raison d'etre*—the only purpose of our existence, the DNA of our Methodist heart. For with the authors of the "Call," we are convinced "that a renewed commitment to the essential principles of scriptural Christianity which we have received in classical Methodist belief, piety, and mission will prepare and strengthen us for the challenges that confront us...." This does not mean cultic preservation centered in tribal traditions and taboos, for it is always unmitigated tragedy to turn our treasures into relics. But this does mean principled fidelity, unswerving devotion and unrelenting purpose all invested in unselfish service to Christ, to His Church, and to the world for which He died.

"We know the power and devastation of sin, and we acknowledge the increasing degradation of our culture," as the "Call" insists. "We are Wesleyans, however; and as our theologians have said, the keynote of our theology is not 'the pessimism of [fallen] nature' but the 'optimism of grace.'" It is this grace so freely offered from the Father's loving heart that provides the holiness that He requires and that we preach. It is this "optimism of grace," so characteristic of our movement at its best, that must ignite us again with the Spirit's power and purpose to escape the irrelevance and disintegration that have faced so many other "holiness movements" before us. Otherwise, like them, we will become merely another sad display in the museum of lost religious causes.

So again we ask, *"What of the future?"* That question may well be answered by what we do with the appeals addressed to us in the "Call to the Conservative Holiness Movement." For cogently and forcefully they point the way to what we can become again—a vital, healthy and flourishing spiritual force ministering to our families, changing our neighborhoods, and impacting our culture. Let's look again at the nine specific "Calls" that have preceded this final one, noting that each of them *affirms, warns* and *calls* us to a scriptural and Wesleyan model of renewal.

1. ***Biblical Fidelity,*** *affirming* devotion to "the Holy Scriptures, as the inspired and inerrant Word of God"; *warning* of focusing on issues and demands "which we cannot legitimately establish from the Scriptures"; and *calling* for "renewed submission to the absolute authority of the Bible, not as a revered icon but as the touchstone for both our personal lives and our public proclamation."

2. ***Historic Roots and Continuity,*** *affirming* "allegiance to the classical Christianity of the centuries, confessing its faith, sharing its historic witness, living out its godly discipline, and claiming all of its treasures as our own"; *warning* of historical ignorance, sectarian bigotry, and spiritual isolation; and *calling* for a "'league offensive and defensive with every soldier of Christ,' reclaiming the richness of our Christian heritage and our essential unity with all who truly confess Him as Lord."

3. ***Christian Community,*** *affirming* our unity with Christ's visible church, "the community of the faithful" in which the "pure Word of God is preached and the sacraments duly administered according to Christ's ordinance"; *warning* us of "a narrow and individualistic approach to our Christian Faith"; and *calling* "for renewed understanding of the Biblical doctrine of the Church as the pillar and ground of the

truth,' reverence for its orthodox confessions, submission to its holy discipline, and faithfulness to its common life."

4. ***Christian Holiness,*** *affirming* that holiness of heart and life is the "central idea of Christianity; as God's redemptive purpose for our fallen humanity"; *warning* "that our passion for holiness of heart and life has sometimes been reduced merely to external codes and prohibitions, and 'holier-than-thou' attitudes toward those who differ from us"; and *calling* "to a renewed love for God from which will blossom consistent and winsome lives of holiness," continuing "to accentuate both of the definitive moments we identify as works of divine grace, conversion and entire sanctification, all the while giving proper attention to the progressive growth in grace by the Spirit."

5. ***Methodist Piety,*** *affirming* that earnest personal devotion so characteristic of our spiritual forebears, a devotion grounded in "profound reverence for God" and in "sober and steadfast love" for Him; *warning* that "our appeals to holy conduct ... have often been based more in the impulse to preserve the taboos of our religious subculture than in allegiance to the Word of God and its demands"; and *calling* for return "to our originating commitment to principled covenant with God," based in these three historic commitments: "(1) the renunciation of all known sin; (2) the embracing of all positive virtue, and (3) the faithful practice of the means of grace, especially ... the Word, prayer, fasting, Christian fellowship and the Lord's Supper."

6. ***Authority in the Church,*** *affirming* that Christ "has delegated the powers of government to duly appointed

officers in the Church ..."; *warning* against "the spirit of autonomy and even anarchy which so often has marked our movement"; and *calling* "for renewed exposition of the Scriptural qualifications for leadership within the Church, corporate exhortation to beware the deceitfulness of sin, and Biblical obedience and submission to those whom God has made under shepherds over us."

7. ***Corporate Worship,*** *affirming* corporate worship of the Holy Trinity as "the exalted glory and central pulse of every Christian congregation...to be conducted with decency and order"; *warning* of overemphasis on the subjective and emotional to the neglect of the solid and objective; and *calling* for "the renewal of our corporate worship, based in the mandates of Scripture and in the tradition of evangelical orthodoxy, centered in the faithful ministry of Word and Sacrament."

8. ***Consistent Discipleship,*** *affirming* Christ's mandate "to make disciples through Trinitarian baptism and instruction in all His commands"; *warning* that "we have largely abandoned our Methodist system of spiritual formation and forgotten how to fulfill our Lord's command to make disciples. We have emphasized spectacular conversions and neglected the Biblical necessity of disciplined growth in faith, virtue, knowledge, self-control, perseverance, godliness, brotherly kindness and love"; and *calling* for a "commitment to equip our laity for the work of the ministry, for the establishment of solidly Wesleyan curricula for systematic discipleship, and for the implementation of these training methods in all our churches."

9. ***Christian Social witness,*** *affirming* that true holiness demands that we follow Jesus who "ministered to both the spiritual and physical needs of people"; *warning* against withdrawal from society with its suffering and loss "into the cloistered walls of a narrow and narcissistic piety"; and *calling* us to "lovingly and forcefully proclaim Christ's power to liberate from sin, both public and private, asserting the claims of His Kingdom against all that militates against it."

In North America and Europe, at least, the Church has its back to the world. But that has happened again and again throughout history; and in every case God has summoned men and women to band together in fervent prayer, renewed commitment and vigorous witness to His truth. With His help and intervention, they have become "storm centers" of revival and revitalization; and in doing so, they have saved the Church from irrelevance and the culture from disintegration. The "Call to the Conservative Holiness Movement" points the way for us to do the same. Let me appeal to all of us—leaders and followers, clergy and lay people, young and old—to consider the "Call" and its nuanced summons and respond affirmatively, vigorously and decisively. We ignore this opportunity at our peril. "Upon the original foundations of our movement, therefore, we must build determined, effective, and contemporary witness to God's unchanging summons to holy hearts and holy lives."

Yes, the message of the final triumph flashes all along the line from Heaven to earth. Granted, this often seems obscured by the descending fog of discouragement and disarray that surround us. But as the "Call" declares, "We cannot cower before the darkness, paralyzed by 'the encircling gloom' which continually we must confront. *'But where sin abounded, grace did much more abound.'* With glad-